AFTER MORE BLACK COFFEE

BOOKS BY ROBERT I. GANNON

After Black Coffee
The Poor Old Liberal Arts
The Technique of the One-Act Play
The Cardinal Spellman Story
After More Black Coffee

AFTER MORE BLACK COFFEE

Robert I. Gannon

NEW YORK
Farrar, Straus and Company

Library of Congress catalog card number 64–23124

First Printing, 1964

Published simultaneously in Canada by
Ambassador Books, Ltd., Toronto.

MANUFACTURED IN THE UNITED STATES OF AMERICA

To My Father 1851-1922

CONTENTS

III

THE EDUCATIONAL PICTURE

IV

A LITTLE IRISH PREJUDICE

Contents

V

AFTERMATHS OF WAR

PREFACE

Eighteen years ago *After Black Coffee,* the predecessor to *After More Black Coffee,* appeared at the urgent request of a Fordham boy who was going into the publishing business. The idea of preserving after-dinner speeches was so outrageous that no one else had ever thought of doing it, and its very impudence was responsible for six printings.

Of course once they were in circulation, the twenty-one masterpieces involved could never be foisted on another American audience, so that still more and more fascinating speeches had to be contrived. In the meantime, the bad habit of taping everything, no matter how illiterate, was spreading rapidly, and soon not only the pulpits but all of the head tables in the country were bugged. It became impossible for a man to get full value out of a spontaneous remark by repeating it half a dozen times. Thus it was that a busy speaker's desk became cluttered with unusable tapes and records and outlines, dusty and dead.

Recently, the suggestion was made that it would be a violation of holy poverty for the oldest man alive to throw all this material in the basket while the Jesuit Foreign Missions stand a chance of dipping into another thousand yen. So twenty-one of the tapes and records were selected, put into English and arranged in some sort of order. The apparent unity, I am afraid, is specious. It is true that most of the comments center on the causes and effects of the second phase in a world war that is still going strong after fifty years. The wisdom offered touches all bases—educational, historic, religious and political. Even the Council gets in on the act. It is so wonderful to be able to offer the solution of all the world's problems! But as it turns out, even that is not enough. The whole picture of the human race in our time gets just a little too depressing without the Irish, and the Irish are no problem at all. So that the unity which might have been found in "problems proposed and solved" has been compromised by an occasional touch of the green.

I

THE COUNTRY WE LIVE IN

A Pluralistic Nation

National Conference of Christians and Jews,
New York, 1962

IT IS not often that an occasion and a subject are so perfectly matched. Get the National Conference of Christians and Jews together, select a field of discussion that is peculiarly their own, and then look for a new angle. Naturally, you will come up with "Jesuits in a Pluralistic Society." All you need then is an old-fashioned Thanksgiving luncheon to give it a flavor and the rest is easy.

There is still some doubt with regard to the debated question, "Who first celebrated Thanksgiving Day?" and I think we should let Virginia and Massachusetts fight it out. In either case, the Protestants deserve the credit but Maimonides and St. Thomas Aquinas would both have agreed that it was a great idea. It is a holiday beloved by all alike, and until the United States Supreme Court gets another scruple the President will go on with his proclamation and all Americans can thank God together even if we are a pluralistic society.

Pluralistic is an old word with a new meaning, like "Dialogue." Look it up in any but the most recent reference works and you will find that it used to mean the opposite of monism or in another connection, possessed of two benefices. Today it means, "a society in which many faiths freely coexist, and in which the rights of religion and private conscience are freely guaranteed." It is no surprise to find that at the first Thanksgiving Day in 1621 there was no such term. No such ideal was recognized. Religious bitterness was at its height and everywhere religious rights were guaranteed only to the dominant party. Catholics had no rights in Protestant countries. Protestants had no rights in Catholic countries. Jews had no countries of their own, so Jews had no rights.

Yet only ten years later in 1631 people were thinking seriously about a pluralistic society, among them the English Jesuits. Even today, some people are surprised that any body of men as uncompromisingly devoted to the Holy See as the Society of Jesus could even grasp the ideals of the Conference of Christians and Jews. They would find it hard to believe that the Jesuits in Maryland were talking the language of the Conference three hundred and thirty years ago.

Dr. Finkelstein, the learned director of the Jewish Theological Seminary, has said that the three most abused terms in the English language are: Pharisaism, Puritanism and Jesuitism. Certainly the use of the third by English writers has seldom implied a compliment. Our Fathers have been blamed for just about every calamity since 1540. In modern times, they started the Franco-Prussian War, the Chicago fire, and several panics. They were at the bottom of the Dreyfus affair and supervised the assassinations of three Presidents. According to Ludendorff, they led the Archduke Francis Ferdinand to Sarajevo and had him murdered by freemasons. All in all, they've been a busy little group.

So in England, under Elizabeth and James I, we got the blame for everything including the Gunpowder Plot. That was why when George Calvert, a friend of the Jesuits, became a Catholic, everyone was amazed that he did not lose the royal favor. The King kept him in the Privy Council, made him Baron of Baltimore in the Kingdom of Ireland and eventually granted him proprietary rights in Maryland.

For the preparation of his charter, the new Lord Baltimore called in three Jesuit advisers. One was Father Henry More, the great-grandson of St. Thomas More. From the outset all were agreed that the general object was to stress the *rights* of Magna Carta rather than the grievances of the barons.

These rights were natural rights, familiar since the Middle Ages. But the Jesuits brought up on Suárez and Bellarmine, emphasized the rights of the people rather than the Divine Right of Kings. Bellarmine had written, "The interests of the Sovereign should be subordinated to the interests of the people. Civil sovereignty comes directly to the people through the Natural Law." So in the Maryland Charter, reflecting this Jesuit thinking, we read that the lawmaking powers of the proprietary are to be exercised, "with the advice, consent and approbation of the freeman."

More interesting still were the Jesuit views on religious rights in a pluralistic society. They were way ahead of their times. They realized that the "New World" was not Catholic or Protestant. It belonged equally to everyone, so it was determined, "Every man might be what religion he pleased and might endeavor to draw others to it by the force of argument and modest ways but without bitterness towards those of other opinions." When the document mentioned "Holy Church" the term was not defined as the Catholic Church. It was not defined at all. For the first time in a bitter century, Catholics and Protestants were to cooperate in a great project, and the thinking of the first Lord Baltimore, influenced by the Jesuits he consulted, was to establish the principles of a pluralistic society and make Maryland the cradle of religious freedom in America. Massachusetts may brag of the *Mayflower* as the symbol of independence, but the symbol of freedom will always be the Ark and the Dove.

This pluralistic society beginning in Maryland as Christian is Christian no longer. Neither is it a Society of Christians and Jews. Too large a proportion of Americans are neither and their number is increasing. So the ideal in our time is logically extended to allow a man of no religion to remain such without becoming a second-class citizen.

With non-religion we can live in peace and mutual charity, realizing that Faith comes to us as a gift, not as the conclusion of a syllogism. Our problem is the antireligion we are meeting at home and abroad; the spirit that scorns and hates and persecutes anybody who believes in God. At home, it is still just an odor. Abroad, it is a poisonous fog that has already enveloped a third of the habitable earth. When Voltaire got a pike in his hand, blood flowed in Europe for fifty years. When Marx got an atomic bomb to work with, the whole world awoke to the possibility of annihilation.

As usual, some good has come out of much evil. Men of good will in every religion have come to acknowledge their real enemy and the fact that this enemy is a real enemy of every other man of good will no matter what his religion. This, more than any other factor, it seems to me, has strengthened the ecumenical spirit of today. Catholics, Protestants and Jews are much closer together than had seemed possible only a few years ago—let us say thirty-four years ago. This indirect reference to the Smith campaign is occasioned by the release the other day of the report drawn up the Fair Campaign Practices Committee. It tells us that the volume of anti-Catholic literature in the Kennedy campaign was many times greater than in 1928. Religious bitterness was better organized than ever before but much less successful. And the reason? More Americans can now admire a fellow American who practices a religion different from their own.

In this, we Catholics find our model in good Pope John, whose circle of friendship includes men of every faith. For him this is no new development of policy. Back in the thirties when he was the Apostolic Delegate in Istanbul, he paid a quasi official visit to the Phanar, the headquarters of the Greek Orthodox Patriarch Benedict II, to announce the election of Pope Pius XII. Such a courtesy had not been customary since the time of Photius, or at least since the Council of Florence. He thought nothing of going to Mount Athos and other Orthodox monasteries to consult their libraries and venerate their icons. Later in Paris, he was the official observer of the Holy See at UNESCO, and, opening the first meeting, gave them a keynote worth remembering.

"We ought to be able," said he, "to have self-respect without being defiant—to get closer to our fellow men without fear—to let ourselves be convinced by others without fearing compromise." He ended with the words: "We shall follow this good road together."

Two of his best friends in the French government were the President, a Socialist and a former Marxist, Vincent Auriol, and the Premier, René Mayer, a freemason and a Jew. So on his election as Pope John XXIII it was expected that the latch would be out at the Vatican for a wide variety of callers, and no one was surprised to see him surrounded one day by eighteen Buddhist monks. He talked to them like their father. He told them that Catholics and Buddhists work for peace, seek the betterment of man and the glory of God. Of course there was not even a hint of indifferentism, but if the missionaries of the sixteenth century could have been present they would have thought that the Pope had left the Church.

So now the Council is upon us, and the eyes of the world are on the Council. At the opening session, good Pope John outlined its four purposes. One of them sounds like the purpose of the National Conference of Christians and Jews, for the Bishops were told that they had gathered in Rome to "make it clear to everyone that each and every person is our brother and our friend."

A United Nation

The Community Chest, Dallas, Texas, 1959

THE time has come to think big thoughts even outside of Texas. Horizons are vanishing, and as outer space becomes more familiar to us, the earth seems to shrink. In the time that it would have taken your grandfathers to travel from Dallas to the Red River, you can make New York; and your children are talking confidently about honeymooning on the moon.

As a result of this sort of progress, some people have lost faith in the importance of man. Dizzy with distances that are measured in light years, they think of man as a microscopic germ crawling on an insignificant satellite, and smile at the idea of his having an immortal soul so important that God would care whether he saved it or not. Other people are affected differently. As the earth shrinks around them, they are conscious of having more neighbors. The speeding up of communications means that there is less reason for parochialism in American life. There is less room than there used to be for religious wars and race wars and class wars. Everything we do now seems to have farther-reaching effects than it used to have. The Community Chest is one example of this. We collect for the neighborhood and benefit the whole country.

The present campaign is a big campaign: 7,000 volunteers, 250,000 givers in a city of 600,000, and a goal of $3,000,000. These figures are constant. They will increase only as Dallas grows in population. But one idea behind the Community Chest has already grown without reference to the city's importance. Your obvious and immediate purpose is to help others, especially to relieve suffering and to give your youngsters a chance to be first-class Americans. That purpose does not change, but another has entered your consciousness. What is steadily growing is the realization that you are meeting a national crisis and helping yourselves and the whole United States not by what you collect as much as by the very act of collecting.

Last year about one-third of the money allocated from the Chest went for health. We are so proud of our American hospitals. They are the envy of the world, and Dallas has some of the finest. We have come a long way, indeed, since the first one in the Western Hemisphere was opened in Mexico City, a hundred years before the *Mayflower* sailed. And we've come farther still since the first one recorded in history. And where was that, did you say? In Ireland, of course, where Princess Macha of the Golden Hair gathered the ailing together nineteen hundred years before Cromwell was born! Today our care of the sick is a model of efficiency, and to us who are writing the last paragraphs of our autobiographies, it is consoling to know that doctors and nurses have all the latest equipment at hand for any emergency. Our only worry is that when the blessed time comes for us to go to our reward, they won't let us die! The problem of overpopulation is not an excess of babies who are full of promise, but of old gaffers of my vintage who have given up promising anything but have to stay around as long as the oxygen holds out.

Even more important then for the future are the family and youth services, which receive two-thirds of your contributions. The precarious state of the American home with its alarming rate of divorce is chiefly a religious and moral problem, but there are many ways in which social agencies, aided by the Community Chest, can help. The same is true of juvenile delinquency, which is so intimately bound up with the decline of family life. For details about our shortcomings and failures in this sphere, we are not dependent on the stories our enemies write in *Trud* and *Izvestia*. They always exaggerate our faults to the point of absurdity. But we have to take seriously the annual reports of J. Edgar Hoover, which emphasize the percentage increase, year by year, of juvenile crime. The stories told by the F.B.I. can often loosen purse-strings for the Community Chest that might not be too affected by an appeal from the Red Cross or the local board of health.

So far, we have dealt with the obvious purpose of the Community Chest in its distribution of funds. Equally important and sometimes overlooked, is the by-product of the whole process: the promotion of American unity—an ideal that means so much in our struggle to survive as a free country. This is part, of course, of the contemporary fight for men's minds.

The fight for men's minds is the second oldest fight in the history of the human race. The oldest is the fight for men's souls. That began when man began. Both fights have been carried on all through history with unabated vigor, and usually so related in their motives as to be carelessly identified. Men have fought for other men's minds in order to save or ruin their souls. At other times, men have fought to save or ruin the souls of men in order to influence their thinking. The patriarchs and prophets were fighting for men's minds; so were the philosophers of early Greece. The first three centuries of Christianity witnessed a battle royal between a totalitarian state and minds which had heard the Good Tidings of man's dignity. Through succeeding centuries details changed frequently, but the main issue has been extraordinarily constant, namely, whether men were to be herds of cattle or human persons.

Today, the struggle is as fierce as ever, the issue the same. Depending on the point of view, people may speak of it as the struggle between spirituality and materialism, religion and paganism, democracy and totalitarianism, East and West, and even between communism and capitalism, but the conflict is being waged at home and abroad. Outside the walls, the slave peoples of the Soviet and her satellites are ranged against the more or less free peoples of the West. Inside the walls, the enemies of human dignity are fighting to win the minds of men to slavery, and here the slogan is as usual—"Divide and conquer." The only part of the world in which this internal struggle is unknown is the other side of the Iron Curtain, where they have achieved a species of quiet—the quiet of a morgue. In a successful police state, fight is unnecessary; there are no minds to fight for. But the rest of the world is a battlefield, even the United States of America. Here the fight is waged on many levels, of which the most obvious may be the economic, but the most important is the moral and religious, because these United States of ours ought to be a religious country. It was discovered and settled by religious men. The Founding Fathers were religious men.

Today, however, it is discouraging to realize how we look to others—the "ugly Americans" seem to be all over the world—and even more discouraging, to realize how we look to ourselves. The picture we get of ourselves in TV, the press, the streets, the theaters, the schools, the courts, the taverns, is not what it should be. Many elements enter into this situation, but one of them is without any doubt our lack of unity. In our efforts to straighten out and be the moral as well as the financial leaders of the world, we find ourselves paralyzed by group hate. This is our nearest and worst enemy. It is not only immoral but irrational. And what does this group hate paralyze first? Our patriotism.

For patriotism with us is not a mere matter of emotion, of marching and flag waving and shaking our fists at other men. It is like religion—an exercise of the intellect and the will. I ask myself, "Do you see the relationship of complete dependence between the Creator of all and you—one of His creatures? Then act as if you did and you will be practicing religion." So too I can say, "Do you see the relationship of partial dependence between you and your country? Then act as if you did and you will be patriotic." Of course my country is not a geographical unit made up of the Great Lakes and the boundless ranches of Texas. It is best defined as the moral union of families all around me who are working for the good of all—for my good. You are my country and my dependence on you is constant. You create public order, without which it would be so much more difficult for me to save my soul. When each of us realizes his dependence on all the rest it makes us conscious of a bond of mutual gratitude that is much more important than any difference that may exist.

As with patriotism, so with treason. The implications of treason go far deeper than its derivation or its legal definition. The word is derived from *traditio,* a "handing over," but many things can be handed over besides the plans for an intercontinental rocket. Its legal definition in the U.S.A. is explicit: "Treason consists in levying war against the United States, in adhering to their enemies giving them aid and comfort." But levying war against my country need not involve guns and uniforms and physical sabotage. What could give more aid and comfort to the enemy today than to know that Americans are attacking that very unity of American families which constitutes the essence of our country; shattering the religious and racial unity of our neighbors; shattering our industrial peace?

In the next phase of this world war that has been dragging on now, hot and cold, since 1914, our principal concern will not be external, mechanical, or financial. We still believe that in such matters "anything they can do, we can do better." We shall be concerned chiefly about the imponderables: about such things as congressional wisdom, industrial honesty, military morale, but first of all about national unity. How, then, can we defend ourselves against the treason of division?

A United Nation

Through the autumn months of 1947 a great public symbol of right thinking was moving along the rails of the country in a kind of triumphal progress. It was called "The Freedom Train." Of all the precious contents that thrilled young America at that time with a sense of its inheritance, none surpassed in popularity the Declaration of Independence. Hundreds of thousands bared their heads, old gray heads and tousled young heads, as they read the words "We hold these truths to be self-evident, that all men are created equal, that they are endowed by their Creator with certain unalienable rights, that among these are life, liberty and the pursuit of happiness."

"All men"—Catholic, Protestant, Jew, black and white and yellow and brown, employer and employee.

"Are created"—made, that is, by God out of nothing so that no one of them has anything to brag about except that for some mysterious reason God wanted him on earth.

"Are created equal"—not physically, mentally or morally but spiritually, that is, as persons, not just as units in a census; as spiritual substances capable of liberty because we can reason about a choice; as unique substances because each person is unlike any other in the world.

In recent years, unfortunately, this American tradition had begun to grow perceptibly dim, especially among the so-called liberal groups that swarmed in the universities before Pearl Harbor. These began by sneering at the Creator and then at the special dignity of human personality. It was not long before they denied liberty as the right of the human person and made him absolutely subject to society. The fact that in doing so they tore up the Declaration of Independence did not bother too many people a few years ago.

But a world war, hot and cold, and the sight of a civilization falling apart have made us very conscious as a nation of our fundamentals. The Declaration of Independence may be just one beloved expression of our way of life, but in teaching us to treat one another as persons it has given us the key to all the disgraceful modern problems that involve Protestants, Catholics, Jews, white and colored people, native born and foreign born, labor and management.

Personality, not sociality, was the foundation of our Republic, and the return of respect for persons is necessary to achieve domestic or international peace. For personality brings God back into the picture. Personality presupposes spirituality, since a person differs from a wolf in the pack in this alone—that he can reason with universal ideas, an activity that rises above the power of matter.

And what is more conducive to seeing God in my neighbor than to work with my neighbor when my neighbor is at his best? Then Americans of every religion and color and of every walk of life do well to put a red feather in their hats and unite at least once a year for the benefit of the community. What they collect is good, but the fact that they collect it together is even better, for the very act of collecting shoulder to shoulder builds up what we need most today—American unity.

A Christian Nation?

The Kerby Foundation, Syracuse, New York, 1959

IN THIS age of "Foundations Explosion" when a hundred new ones are set up every year to escape some phase of the income tax, it is consoling to read the sources and the purposes of the William J. Kerby Foundation. When the friends and admirers of this great Monsignor gathered the funds together, their interest was not to keep them away from the government but to give them back to the government in a different form: in the form of moral strength and prestige. They wanted to promote "a deepening awareness of the spiritual basis of our democratic institutions—and the importance of religion to stimulate respect for the dignity and rights of the individual."

They have not spelled it out, perhaps, but it should be clear that the kind of democracy they are promoting is not the pagan democracy of the French Revolution. It is rather the democracy that came to the Fathers of our country in 1789 from the Fathers of the early church through the channel of medieval English law. It is a Christian democracy.

I realize the risk we take when we become explicit. Some of our leading statesmen have stirred up hornets' nests by taking risks like that. There was the case of President Harry S. Truman. I doubt if the incident is included in his official biography, but it was significant enough to analyze on an occasion like this. Back in the summer of '47 he was reappointing Myron Taylor as his personal representative at the Vatican and wrote to Pius XII what his advisers regarded as a cordial and harmless letter:

"As the chosen leader of the people of the United States I am privileged to pledge full faith to you once again to work with your Holiness and every agency of good the world over for an enduring peace.

"An enduring peace can be built only upon Christian principles. To such a communication we dedicate all our resources, both spiritual and material, remembering always that 'except the Lord build the house, they labor in vain who build it.'

"Your Holiness, this is a Christian nation. More than half a century ago, that declaration was written into the decrees of the highest court in this land. As a Christian nation our earnest desire is to work with men of good-will everywhere."

There was an immediate outcry from some of our fellow citizens. Mr. William Lieberman, for example, a Brooklyn lawyer who was twice delegate to the National Republican Convention, wrote a blistering article in the *Jewish Forum* calling for the impeachment of the President. It was a campaign document, and not one of the classics in that emotional field. It does not awaken any echoes of "The Letters of Junius" and probably had no effect on the vote, but it is still helpful in clarifying our thinking on certain points.

Coming from a lawyer, we might expect a few ifs and ands, but this attack was sweeping. Mr. Lieberman found Mr. Truman's letter "completely false and offensive." The United States, he said, was in no sense a Christian nation. Nowhere was such a declaration written into the decrees of the highest court in the land. Enduring peace could be built on other than Christian principles. And as for the President, in making such statements he violated the United States Constitution by breaching the wall of separation between Church and State. Was somebody in the White House reading the wrong book or was it Mr. Lieberman? Let us check the indictment point by point.

When the prosecuting attorney says that nowhere is such a declaration written into the decrees of the Supreme Court, he seems to be correct. With all his conspicuous virtues it must be admitted that Mr. Truman has been at times somewhat on the impulsive side. A little "red herring" may someday be carved on his headstone. In the present instance he was thinking of the opinion written by Mr. Justice Brewer, back in the early nineties in *Holy Trinity vs. the United States,* and he may not have noticed that the justice in turn was quoting from another case—*Uptigraph vs. the Commonweal of Pennsylvania.* So that his words rate as an *obiter dictum,* not as a decree from the highest court in the land. That means that we have to begin by chalking one up for Mr. Lieberman.

On the other points raised, he is not so fortunate. Take that one on enduring peace being built on other than Christian principles. Mr. Truman had written, "These moral principles are in the hearts of good men the world over. They are in all churches and schools." He was not then referring to principles peculiar to Christianity but compatible with it. He was referring to the dignity of man as a person and to the supremacy of law over the ruler. So too when Mr. Lieberman speaks of a violation of the Constitution and the imaginary wall that separates Church and State, we can laugh it off as the fine frenzy of a Republican in a presidential year. Clearly, there was no question of the country being Christian by law established but just in certain accepted senses.

These certain senses are what bring us now to the principal point: Is it true that the United States is not in any sense a Christian nation? Some Catholics would say that it is not Christian because its specific end is not religious. That does seem pretty technical, doesn't it? Others would say that it is not a nation at all but just a continent in the process of growing into a community with no common past, just a common future. I wonder. It is true that we have no common origin, no common stock, tradition or religion as European nations have or have had. But we have the strong bond of nine generations living and working together for the good of all. So assuming that we are a nation, are we "in any sense a Christian nation"?

We certainly are not a Christian nation by law established like England, Sweden or Spain. Everyone who has read the American Bill of Rights knows that "Congress shall make no law respecting an establishment of religion," and if Congress doesn't do it, nobody else can. In certain recent controversies, some seem to have thought with Bishop Oxnam that the framers of the Constitution were anticipating an attack from the "Pope of Rome," but of course what they had in mind was that the Established Church of England was to be established here no more, nor was any other to take its place. The Constitution was reasonable enough and clear enough, but the lengths to which the present members of the United States Supreme Court have gone in stretching and torturing its obvious intent is a matter of grave concern to many.

Perhaps, however, we are Christians on the basis of population. Certainly there was a time when that could be accepted as a fact. In the President's words: "It is not without significance that the valiant pioneers who left Europe to establish settlements here at the very beginning of their Colonial enterprises declared their faith in the Christian religion and made ample provision for its practices and its support. The story of the Christian missionaries who in the earliest days endured hardships, even death itself, in carrying the Message of Jesus Christ to untutored savages is one that still moves the hearts of men."

We were still a Christian people when the time came for George Washington to resign as Commander in Chief of the Army. Speaking to the governors of the thirteen new states, he said: "I now make it my earnest prayer that God would graciously be pleased to dispose us all to do justice and love mercy and to demean ourselves with that charity, humility and pacific temper of the mind which were the characteristics of the Divine Author of our Blessed Religion, without a humble imitation of whose example in these things, we can never hope to be a happy nation." Thus he assumed that the thirteen governors believed with him that the future happiness of the U.S.A. depended upon the imitation of Christ. If then we are Christian in origin at least, it cannot be said that we are "in no sense a Christian nation."

But are we today as Christian as we used to be? Unfortunately no. Mr. Lieberman is not far from the truth when he says that "fifty-six per cent of our people are unchurched and sixty per cent unbaptized." A great and growing section of the population still talk and look like Christians but reject or at least ignore essential Christian doctrine.

What about American philosophy? Is it Christian? Is it anything? The winds have blown across our continent the influences of just about every school in Europe, not to speak of the Orient. We have had our materialists, our Cornell idealists, and our logical empiricists. Any list of American philosophers would certainly begin with William James, Whitehead, Norbridge, Santayana, Cohen and Dewey. So that, in spite of a liberal sprinkling of neo-Thomists in and out of the Church, no one could call the philosophy of the United States, Christian.

What about our education? Like the nation itself, our education is Christian in its origin. All our venerable institutions, with the exception of the University of Virginia, were founded by Christians. The prime object of most of them was the training of the clergy. But when our future leaders began taking their doctorates in France and Germany, too many came home with the express purpose of driving Christ out of higher education. Their success at the university level has found an echo today even in the grammar grades.

What then of our moral ideals? Can we be brief on this depressing aspect? A public examination of conscience would be rather out of place at this genial dinner. J. Edgar Hoover's regular reports underlining the percentage increase of crime, especially of juvenile crime, are enough to establish this much of Mr. Lieberman's claim. Our moral ideals are certainly no longer Christian.

Oddly enough, our political ideals present a brighter picture. In this field our heritage is practically intact. Our ideal of democracy is still the medieval ideal, the Christian ideal of the Founding Fathers. It still rests securely on two really Christian principles: the first of these, the supremacy of the law over the ruler, finds its basis in English common law, the law of custom and tradition. Asking, as it always does, "What have our ancestors regarded invariably as just and unjust?", it presupposes another law that springs from our very nature as rational creatures. This is a Divine Law, known through human reason, older than any man-made law and superior to it.

Before the Christian era, no one had ever recognized anything of the kind. The Jews had divine positive law known by revelation and collected into codes. Such were the Ten Commandments. The pagans had human positive law created by state edict and also collected into codes. But the American concept, which endures even today, of a natural law binding rulers and ruled, to which all positive law must conform, leads back through our own John Marshall and James Wilson to Edmund Burke, Lord Somers, Seldon and medieval lawyers like Henry de Bracton; back beyond Magna Carta to St. Ambrose and St. Augustine.

The same can be said of the American ideal of equality. It is not related to the *Egalité* of the French Revolution. That was inspired by the pagan Stoics and denied all inequalities of any kind. Equality in the American Constitution is specific. It springs from the fact that men are persons—that is, individuals with spiritual powers—adopted sons of God. It is because they are persons that no man has the right to impose his will on another except as God's representative. This tradition may be attacked as unfair to atheists. It suggests a crack in the wall that separates Church and State. It might even embarrass Mrs. McCollum's little boy as much as having his classmates instructed in religion, out in Champaign, Illinois, but it is hard to declare a tradition which gave rise to the Constitution, unconstitutional. In its ideals of democracy, then, the United States is still a Christian country.

All in all, President Truman was not too far off the beam. We admit that there has been no decree from the highest court in the land that we are officially Christian and that unfortunately we no longer think and behave like Christians, but because of our origins and our ideals of democracy no one can say, without being challenged, that the United States of America is "not in *any sense* a Christian nation."

An Immigrant Nation

The American-Irish Historical Society, New York, 1954

WE HAVE been celebrating in the privacy of our family prayers the centenary of the Great Migration—the migration of the Irish people to America. Some of the blessed race, of course, had been here from the earliest time. But it was, after all, the decade from 1848 to 1858 that saw the Great Migration, that saw a million and a half of Erin's sons and daughters leaving their most distressful country and asking a mother's welcome from a strange if happier land. Classified at first as low-grade wool, they have woven themselves with all their warm color, their shining devotion to God, their sparkling wit into the warp and woof of American life. With all their faults, and we can credit them with having at least half as many as the English, they have made America a grander, brighter, freer place to live in.

This led your distinguished President to suggest that since Ambassador Taft* would discuss weightier aspects of Ireland's history in the principal address of the evening, and since I was not allowed to confine myself to a few words of sincere gratitude for making me the medalist of the year, I might open a brief and informal discussion on the subject of this great migrating group by taking one sample for examination and following a particular but typical family through five generations.

Old John Malone—Lord John, the neighbors called him be-

* William Howard Taft, U.S. Ambassador to Ireland.

cause of his arrogance—was born in 1798 and became the manager of an English landlord's estate on the Shannon River near Elphin. There he lived until 1896, when visitors from America found him still dressed in shoe buckles and knee pants, still laying down the law to his neighbors. His only son, another John, was handsome and strong, but something like his father in disposition, hard and stubborn. When he was twenty-one, he heard that his father intended to marry again in defiance of a very deep and very old Irish prejudice. So after a few hot words on the subject, he walked over to French Park and asked Mary Clancy if she would marry him and go to New York. Mary was smart enough to say yes. How much, if anything, the Great Famine had to do with their decision I never learned, because the stress was always laid on the old man's unseasonable romance. He must have been all of forty-five at the time. Mary was as strong a character as John, but more intelligent, more amiable and a little on the leisurely side. All through her life, which ended in 1890 at the age of fifty-nine, she ruled the family from a rocking chair. She was that familiar type of Irish matriarch who was loved by everybody, even by her in-laws, and was waited on hand and foot by unmarried daughters who were encouraged to think that such was their main vocation in life.

The bride and groom landed in Castle Garden something more than a decade before the Civil War, and instead of settling in the city and going into politics and the contracting business, moved up to Spring Valley in Rockland County, where John got his first American job on the Erie Railroad. Before very long he was made a baggage master and kept the same run from Port Jervis to Jersey City for the next forty years. Meanwhile the Erie shops were moved from Piermont to Port Jervis, and John moved his little family with them, settling on the bluff above the Delaware River in a rambling two-story house which still stands in surprisingly good condition. There Mary presented him with the rest of their thirteen children, and there they lived in peace and sufficiency until the end of the nineteenth century. For a short time they were under a cloud in the parish when word got around that John had left the Democratic Party to vote for Abraham Lincoln. The pastor feared for his faith, and stones were thrown at him in the streets, but John was a stubborn man and it was perhaps as much willfulness as sagacity that kept him a lifelong Republican. But with due allowance for this personal eccentricity, he could be taken, I think, as a typical first-generation Irish American.

His eldest son, Frank, was equally typical of the second generation. After four years of formal schooling and a boyhood of odd jobs to help out the large household, he was considered ready for real work at fifteen. So his father took him over to the roundhouse and introduced him to the foreman, a Roscommon man, who promptly put him to work washing an engine. At the end of one day, however, he wiped his hands and solemnly announced that he would never again so much as touch a piece of waste—and he never did! He took up, instead, what was then the latest thing, a job for a gentleman—telegraphy; and at seventeen he was working at his new profession, dressing carefully and being teased by the Port Jervis Irish for wearing kid gloves. At twenty-one he was a train dispatcher with a very definite idea of what he wanted to be.

Soon after this he was down in the big city where he met a Protestant girl a little younger than himself, whose English grandfather had come over from Birmingham. Her father owned not one but two glass factories and had sent her to school in Packer Institute, which eighty-five years ago was quite the place, in Brooklyn. He had never met anyone like her before. In heart and mind and manners Marietta Burrows had everything that could be asked for in the mother of a large family and the wife of a successful man. What was more important still, she returned his love. So at the age of twenty-three he married her, the day after she was received into the Church by a holy Jesuit! That was in 1874. There were a few holy ones still around.

Together they prospered. A promotion came with every child and they were blessed with nine. Frank rose rapidly from train dispatcher to superintendent, general manager, vice-president, president and chairman of the board. He traveled much, liked good books, good company and good music, so that in spite of the brevity of his schooling, he wrote well, talked well, thought clearly, and had great influence with men. There was no touch of the brogue in his speech and he never set foot on the little green isle, but all his life long he was a sentimental Irishman whose heart was always open to a greenhorn and whose eyes would fill with mist at the first notes of his favorite song, "Believe Me If All Those Endearing Young Charms." Such was the second generation of the Irish in America.

The third generation grew up, eight boys and one girl, unconscious of any hyphen. They all traveled extensively, had the advantage of private schools and the colleges of their choice. Among them was a civil engineer, a lawyer, a doctor, a railroader, two businessmen and a priest. Four of the boys married girls of Irish ancestry. The others introduced new strains into the next generation, notably English, French and Dutch. They all kept the Faith, but not with equal enthusiasm. All but one remained in the Republican Party. They differed on most subjects, but were agreed on this, that no one in the third generation compared in character or ability with their parents—a condition rather typical of third generations in this country.

In the fourth generation there were twenty-six boys and girls, ten of them with as little as one-quarter of Irish blood—most of them unconscious of their links with the County Roscommon, and quite uninterested in anything connected with it. Nineteen have married, but only four married a boy or girl with an Irish name. After a century in America, in spite of one priest and two nuns in the fourth generation, the family begins to show its first cracks in the religious front. There have been a few bad marriages and apparently some doubt with regard to the value of spiritual training, at least at the college level. There is some ignorance too, and a certain lack of simplicity, but no formal repudiation of their heritage, so that eighty-five per cent of the fourth generation deserve the full approval of their Irish forebears.

Now the fifth generation is upon us. To date, there are forty-one of them, the eldest twenty, the youngest a matter of months. It is still too early to note the influence of their environment on their character, but in the matter of mixed strains of blood they are moving still further away from Elphin. Twenty-one have Irish names, but only fifteen have enough royal blood in their veins to be conscious of their superiority. Fortunately, however, a drop is always enough to raise them above the general.

This, then, is the story of one branch of one Irish family that came to America during the Great Migration—a family that, representing in the fifth generation a dozen national strains, has melted completely into the American background without serious damage to the background in the melting process. But this has been more than a family story. It is the story of the Irish in America. A simple, homespun story, it is not too distinguished or heroic, but neither is it too unworthy of those ancestors of ours who kept their integrity through two and one-half centuries of crucifixion and gave their descendants a chance, at least, to inherit some of their fidelity, intelligence and wit. And by the way, the name of the family we analyzed was not Malone at all. What was it now? I've forgotten!

II

MAINLY HISTORICAL

They Live in Us

Annual Dinner, The Sovereign Military Order of Malta, New York, 1963

IT HAS been my honor now for perhaps ten years—man and boy—to attend this impressive dinner, but of course tonight is the big night. Tonight I appear for the first time with a blaze of glory around my neck and I hope that the humble, poverty-stricken Jesuit Saints in Heaven won't disown me when I admit that I had a great time this morning. I felt like a schoolboy going up for his first letter in basketball.

But even without this unexpected and undeserved distinction which makes January 14 one of the very few important dates in my life, just attending another meeting of this Sovereign Order would be a privilege. It may not be the gayest dinner of the year, but to me it has always been the most fascinating. It is so colorful, and, what is more important, so drenched with history.

As for the color, you have no idea how impressive you are from here—at least collectively. Your President Master peers out through the dim candlelight and sees at every table nine Master Knights in golden armor prefected by a bishop, or at least a prothonotary apostolic. They are very young knights indeed who have been assigned nothing better than a college president to impress them. On the dais we have His Eminence. (Isn't it good to have him home again safe and sound? I hope when he gets to be my age he will slow down a little. But maybe he knows what he is doing. Starting out on his last trip, he looked as if he was going to be buried at sea. But he dashed around the world in the middle of winter, shook hands with several thousand people and came back looking as young as a Very Reverend Monsignor.) So here he is, beaming as usual in his cardinalitial purple—a wonderful color that was designed originally to make the bishops look as if they were doing penance. The only man I ever saw who could distract attention from a Prince of the Church was our own hereditary marquis, George MacDonald. When he got everything on, he could outshine a Melchite Patriarch. To me, George was a living refutation of the charge sometimes whispered around Europe, that democratic America tends to make light of the traditional qualifications for a Knight of Malta. As you know so well, a candidate for our Sovereign Military Order is expected to be (1) baptized, (2) over twenty-one, (3) without a criminal record, and (4) a member of the nobility of sixteen quarterings. I am not too sure just what a quartering is, and I never counted George's, but he always looked and sounded as if he had at least twenty-six. We have reason to miss him, and we do. In his place, however, we have a President Master who certainly qualifies for any listing of nobility, not only because he has always been known as a Prince but by the simple fact that he is a former President of the Friendly Sons of St. Patrick. Now there is aristocracy for you! At their annual solemn conclaves in New York, it is not uncommon for even the wandering minstrels who just tell the jokes to be of royal blood. I don't like to brag, but as a descendant of Spanish kings wrecked off the coast of Galway, I consider myself tonight the representative of the Emperor Charles V, who gave us the Island of Malta in the first place after we were thrown out of Rhodes. Do you realize, gentlemen, that the only order in the Church that has been thrown out of more and better places than we have is the Jesuit Order?

This evening, then, we have no lack of color. Every knight in the room was distinguished in his own right before he was decorated, but what makes this the most interesting group that will dine here during 1963 is that we exemplify a miracle.

The miracle is found in an essentially changeless church which is changing accidentally all the time; which has as many phases as history itself—phases that are as transient as history's own, with this sole difference: no expression of the Church's life down through the ages is ever wholly, heartlessly cast aside but in one way or another is always kept in affectionate remembrance. At the ordination of a deacon, the days of St. Stephen come alive again. At the Kyrie of the Mass, we think of St. Luke and the old Greek Fathers, while the tremendous liturgy of Holy Week is full of the Catacombs. In like manner a group of American business and professional men in evening dress and formal decorations are a living reminder of one of the Church's phases, and through you, we can still see, like giants in the shadows, the knights of the twelfth and thirteenth centuries—Knights of St. John in great black mantles; their deadly rivals, the Templars, in mantles of white; Teutonic Knights; the Knightly Orders of Spain; and all the others which, we are told, were close to a hundred in number.

They were once the glory of the Church and the right arm of their princes because they were the perfect expression of the times that called them into being. They were essentially the outgrowth of great, stirring, bloody, violent days of high idealism.

Our predecessors began with the care of the sick, but the laymen among us, seeing the more glamorous exploits of the Templars in the field, took up arms themselves. It might have been better for Jerusalem and the Church if the Hospitalers had been content to stay in the hospitals, for as long as they were absorbed in Red Cross work and the Templars were winning glory of another kind, there was harmony in the Christian ranks. But when the Hospitalers took up the sword and matched their skill with the Templars in battle, the rival orders came to hate each other more than they did the Saracens. The result was inevitable. The Christians were driven from pillar to post until in 1291 the fall of Acre, their last stronghold, ended for all practical purposes the period of the Crusades.

That, however, was not the end of our beloved order. The bold knights simply changed services and, passing from the army to the navy, they curbed the power of the Saracens on the sea, ransomed slaves and helped Don John of Austria at Lepanto. What really ruined the order in the end—and I don't want to give anybody here any scruples—was its unholy interest in real estate. Eventually the knights were drawing revenue from nineteen thousand estates in Europe alone, where an estate frequently extended over several villages. Then, as if real estate were not dangerous enough, they went into banking. The Knights of Malta became the bankers of Europe centuries before the Rothschilds came on the scene. If there had been a stock exchange in those days, the Grand Knight of Malta would have been its president.

Mention of their financial success is what prepares us for their final disintegration, because on the heels of wealth in the Church, instinct teaches us to look for corruption. Rhodes and later Malta became, in time, scenes of wild brutality and excess. Poverty went first and, as usual, obedience and chastity were not long in following. Malta saw the terrible day when the knights rose in armed revolt against the Grand Master because he proposed to expel lewd women from the commandery, and later, traveling the customary path from broken vows to ruined Faith, they ignored the Pope and elected Czar Paul of Russia to be their head.

But let no one turn his back on them now and leave them in disgrace. The Church herself is much more charitable. If these vanished knights exemplify, through her adaptability, the miraculous and eternal youth of Rome, they offer as well a touching reminder of her sweet old age. She is vigorous. Of course she is. She is militant and as modern as tomorrow. The whole non-

Catholic world has been watching her with wonder during the first session of the present Ecumenical Council, watching her as she proposed to change her armor, her dress, her sensible appeal to save a generation rising in the nuclear age. And yet, she remains at heart a dear old mother with all the tender sentiment of a mother's love. No woman ever treasured the keepsakes of her children's early years with more affection than the Church has always shown. Her liturgy, her prayers, her vestments are thronged with memories. She never quite forgets any chapter of her glorious past, or anyone who was of service to her. That is why our leading laymen can take their places today in her sanctuaries close to the thrones of her bishops wearing the old white cross and bearing the name of a knighthood long since dead.

Dead? Dead is the wrong word for a living body transformed by resurrection. The day of the sword may have passed but not the day of defense. The Church is still facing a critical struggle, a struggle so critical that it dwarfs the old defense of the Holy Places. For the pagan world is growing much faster than the Christian, and in the Christian world disbelief is growing faster than the Faith. In the Catholic Church itself, the laity is growing much faster than the clergy. People talk of the population explosion, but there is no explosion of religious vocations in sight. The fact is that if the present trend continues, the United States may one day face the problem of South America with one priest for every ten thousand Catholics. And then we shall see in other parts of our beloved country what has been familiar so long in Alabama and Texas: Murphys and O'Briens and Sullivans signing up with Jehovah's Witnesses because, years before, there had been no priest around to say Mass for their fathers and mothers. That is why, in the uncertain future that lies ahead of us, the Church will rely more than ever upon well-informed, devoted laymen; laymen worthy to be called its Master Knights; laymen of the type of John S. Burke and Thomas E. Murray—

John and Tom to all of us, who were with us in this very dining room, it seems only yesterday.

It is now the year of Our Lord, 1963. The fierce knights who fought their way from Jerusalem to Rhodes and Malta are not even dust. Their brave swords are not even rust. All their wealth, all their power, all that was material and dragged them down, all that was of the earth, earthy, has fallen away from them into nothingness, leaving behind a kind of purified spirit, an abstraction, an ideal. As a pure ideal they continue to exist in us, and it is thus, as an ideal, that they will always be remembered by their mother who with a true mother's instinct overlooks their sad maturity, when they turned away and walked no more with her, and sees them now as full of life and courage and love as they were when she knew them first, when they looked up into her face with clear-eyed youth, eight hundred years ago.

Isaac Hecker Was a Modern

Centenary of the Society of Missionary Priests of St. Paul the Apostle, New York, 1961

WE ALL think of the Paulist Fathers as being in the tradition of their founder, modern and American, and so they are—but it does take a little practice in historical perspective to realize that an American born 139 years ago can still be called a modern.

Isaac Hecker began life as the contemporary of Queen Victoria. She outlived him, but they were born the same year—1819. Dickens and Thackeray and Browning were just children at the time. Walter Scott was all the rage, and in the world of English poetry it was Keats and Shelley and Byron. The Pope was Pius VII, and now that Napoleon Bonaparte was in exile and the Council of Vienna had met, the Church was enjoying a few years of peace. The United States was still recovering from the War of 1812, which had changed the face of things and not for the better. Jefferson and Carroll and many of the other Founding Fathers were still alive and Commodore Vanderbilt was running the Staten Island ferry. A background of this kind sounds like ancient history, but modern times were just around the corner.

When Isaac's father, who was a metalworker by trade, emigrated from Germany at the turn of the century, workers of all kinds—skilled and unskilled, Catholic, Protestant and Jew—were still welcome in the United States, but when Isaac was nine years old a famous high tariff bill was passed which profoundly affected the labor situation and led in a few years to the ugly crisis of Nativism. Till then, our economics had been spelled out in terms of agriculture, home industry and clipper ships. After the tariff, however, we began to emulate Great Britain which was up to its neck in the wretched social conditions of the Industrial Revolution. The era of factories began, of railroads, coal mines, great private fortunes, and wage slaves. With no unions to fight for them, native workers, the sons and daughters of the American Revolution, were soon in a pitiable condition, uneducated, underpaid and starving. So that when in the thirties and forties and fifties revolution in Germany, together with famine and brutality in Ireland, created great waves of immigration and even lower wages in the United States, the newcomers to this land of opportunity were met with bitterness and prejudice. The fact that most of them were Catholic turned a laborer's resentment into religious hate, leading eventually to the burning of churches and convents.

It was Isaac Hecker's good fortune that although his father was an immigrant and he himself a first-generation German-American, he was born of Protestant parents before the rush began, and that made him a Yankee, welcome in all circles. Even in Boston, where the Athenians regarded the rest of America as a wilderness, this young baker from New York with a very sketchy education was accepted by the Ripleys, the Danas, the Bradfords and the Alcotts. He boarded with Henry Thoreau and visited with George Bancroft and Ralph Waldo Emerson. They never thought of him as the son of a German metalworker, the brother of a couple of German-American bakers who pushed their own carts around Hester Street. They forgot about the hyphen. So did he. For the Heckers had arrived just early enough to join those in possession, to be one of the symbols of Americanism. In time this was to become a cause of some anxiety and misunderstanding because Americanism was the name invented in France for a nonexistent heresy in the United States

—but in the end, the fact that Isaac Hecker was a "Yankee born and bred" proved to be providential in molding the spirit and defining the purpose of the future Paulists.

Convinced as he was from childhood that "God had work for him to do," our Yankee was unhappy in a square paper cap, baking bread with his brothers, and threw himself heart and soul into the cause of the working man, primarily of the native working man. Still in his teens, he joined the Locofocos, a picturesque branch of Tammany Hall. The name had not been invented by Republicans. The boys had wished it on themselves and had organized to oppose money groups, especially banks. Isaac was all for advancing the worker by tearing up paper money and throttling the banker that engraved it. But in 1841 a famous writer and philosopher from Boston, Orestes Brownson, came to town to lecture on equal rights and liberty. Young Hecker was tremendously impressed by the man and carried away by the new conviction that books could do more than ballots in righting human wrongs. As he advanced in the next few years from one mystical experience to another, groping toward the light, he realized that his fellow Americans had needs that were deeper than those that were merely economic or even political. This became still more clear to him after he was received into the Church by Bishop John McCloskey at Old St. Patrick's on Mott Street.

By this time it was evident to all his friends that young Hecker had a vocation to the priesthood, and some of his advisers suggested Fordham where he could study for the diocese of New York. Bishop McCloskey, however, for some mysterious reason, tempted him with the life of St. Ignatius, and someone else sent him out to Holy Cross College in Worcester. Fortunately, however, the Jesuits who had left New York in 1815 did not return till 1846, so the impression they made on the young man was not too distinct. That was providential. Had they been able to snare him, he would have died in the Society. And we? We should not be here celebrating tonight and all the wonderful Paulists would be wasting their time as vice-presidents and directors of athletics at Fordham University. As it turned out, a good old German Redemptorist got hold of him down on Third Street and Avenue A and that settled it. Isaac agreed with him that "the discipline and standards of religion were not so high among the English and the Irish" as they were among the Germans. In those days nobody seemed to like the Irish but the Irish. When Orestes Brownson wrote his famous article branding a section of the Irish Americans as "a miserable rabble," his friend Hecker did not contradict him but told him to watch his step, because so many of the bishops in America were straight from the Old Sod. This general attitude on the part of the young convert did not spring from prejudice against any particular race or nationality, but from the deep conviction that Protestant America would never accept the Catholic Faith from an Irish hierarchy or an Irish clergy. In more general terms, he believed with Orestes Brownson that only native-born Americans could make the Catholic Church acceptable to America, and in this conviction he never wavered. Because of his belief that Providence, as he put it, was calling him to America to convert a certain class of persons among whom he had found himself before his own conversion, he went through a long and heartbreaking struggle, brilliantly described in Father Vincent Holden's book, *The Yankee Paul,* which ended with his parting from the German Redemptorists to organize the first little band of Paulist Fathers at Fifty-ninth Street and Ninth Avenue.

The Americans to whom he dedicated the rest of his life had their virtues and their faults. At their best they were generous and fair-minded. At their worst they could be incredibly blind and bigoted. Father Hecker was ready for every type, and handed on to his sons a fair share of his learning, resourcefulness, spirituality, and, above all, a share of his talent for making everyone feel at home in his Father's House. Like their founder, the Paulists of today specialize in the mental processes of the average American. Like their founder they "help Catholics with their left hand, Protestants with their right." Many of the innovations which they have introduced into missionary work are now so widely adopted in the Church that their origin has been forgotten.

Theirs, for instance, was the first Catholic monthly in America, the learned but popular *Catholic World*—for so many years the externalization of Father James Gillis—and now continued in the best tradition by Father John B. Sheerin. Theirs was the first regular pamphlet service with racks in the back of the church. It is now responsible for the incredible output of five million pamphlets a year. The books published by the Paulist press have reached the impressive total of more than ten million, not counting five million copies of the Army and Navy Prayerbook. When we come to their missions for non-Catholics, their pioneering in radio with the much lamented station WLWL, and their famous information centers where any stranger can drop in and ask about the nuclear weapons that are stored in St. Patrick's Cathedral, the sale of indulgences, the price of absolution, the Jesuit teaching that the end justifies the means; when we check up besides on the admirable results of their forty-two Newman Clubs in various non-Catholic universities, we must echo Archbishop Cushing's remark that their influence in America is out of all proportion to their numbers.

Some say that Isaac Hecker was too optimistic about his great vocation, too much like Cardinal Wiseman who expected England to be Catholic overnight. He seemed so, for example, when he wrote in 1865: "We are only six—two of us quite broken down. A fine set of fellows we are to set on foot the conversion of the country. Don't be alarmed. We have now taken root in eternity, we are not shabbier than the Apostles were in the natural order. If twelve of them were enough to put on foot the conquest of the world, six of us are enough for this continent."

That was expecting a lot, but you can see by his smile that he was joking. He was whistling to keep up his courage at a very discouraging time. Now, however, that a hundred years have passed, we can list more than enough successes in the field to hearten his sons in their present apostolate. Take just the simple statement that last year 140,414 converts were instructed and baptized in the Catholic Church. A surprising proportion of these were due to the direct influence of the Paulist Fathers. How many they influenced indirectly by their hundreds of missions, thousands of conversations and millions of pamphlets and books is beyond calculation. Only the recording angels can say how great the harvest has been.

May I then, in your name, thank God tonight for our own dear Paulist Fathers and for their holy founder, the German-American baker boy whose patriotism was so much a part of his piety.

Fifty Years of Research

The American-Irish Historical Society, New York, 1947

IN 1897 the reading public in the United States knew remarkably little about the Irish. They were newcomers. They made good honest servants. They had infiltrated the police force. They had taken over Tammany Hall. They drank too much. They went to church every Sunday—every single Sunday. They were always in a fight of some kind. They were very funny. It seems there were once two Irishmen, Pat and Mike. . . . And then the reading public began to catch up, partly at least as a result of your scholarly society.

It discovered that the popular song of the day about Columbus coming over here and meeting Mr. Dooley was not too much of an exaggeration. Only a hundred and fifty years after Columbus, in 1643, St. Isaac Jogues set foot on the shore of Manhattan, and one of the two who knelt to ask his blessing was an Irish boy. The trouble was that there were not enough of the Irish in seventeenth-century America for the intellectual good of the country. Our earliest seventeenth-century settlers had come over from various parts of Europe equipped for the most part with a good education. The *Mayflower* and the *Ark* and the *Dove* had a fair sprinkling of Oxford and Cambridge men who brought with them their own plans and aspirations for the schooling of their children. But two or three generations of wood-chopping and fighting Indians did so little for American culture that during the first half of the eighteenth century most of the colonies were such that no conscientious descendant would want his young ancestors turned loose in them. Around the 1740's and 1750's, however, a new stream of immigration began to arrive on our shores—a trickle in 1725, a flood by the middle of the century. It was made up of German farmers from the Palatinate, Scottish Blue Bonnets, and Irish—both Orange and Green—usually in separate ships! The reason for the sudden immigration of the Irish was, incidentally, the same as that in the middle of the nineteenth century. For in 1740 also there was a disastrous potato blight with subsequent famine, only less appalling than the famine that our grandfathers knew. As far as the New World was concerned, however, the misfortune of the Irish was a blessing, for the educational level of this group, as of the others, including the Huguenots who had come a little earlier, was on the whole higher than the general average of American colonials of the day. Some of the Scots were university men and all knew their Bible backwards and were proficient in mathematics—especially in subtraction! The Germans came over with teachers like Pastorius, who knew eight languages and was perhaps the greatest scholar in early colonial history, while the Irish brought their tradition of the famous old Hedge schoolmasters. Most of the latter were bilingual, knew their Gaelic as well as their English, and some of them who had studied in Paris and Salamanca had Latin and Greek and French and Spanish besides. In Ireland there wasn't much they could do with their learning, as Padraic Colum* has phrased it so beautifully:

> Our order broken, they who were our blood
> Knew not themselves the heirs of noted masters,
> Of Columbanus and Erigena;
> We strove towards no high reach of speculation,
> Towards no delivery of gestated dogma,

* A guest of honor at the dinner.

No resolution of age-long dispute.
Only to have a priest beside the hedges,
Baptizing, marrying,
Offering Mass within some clod-built chapel,
And to the dying the last sacrament
Conveying, no more we strove to do—
We, all bare exiles, soldiers, scholars, priests.

But when these scholars trained in the liberal arts came to America, they brought with them heads full of sparks that would add to the approaching conflagration, so that if only poor George III could have been his own grandfather he might have done as he jolly well pleased with his downtrodden provincials. It was the chief misfortune of his unfortunate reign that by 1765 ideas that were not entirely British were beginning to work on the American mind, and when the Declaration of Independence was signed, thirteen of the signers were Irish. They were not all Knights of Columbus—more's the pity—but neither are you, and neither was Robert Emmet or Wolfe Tone!

What part the Irish took in George Washington's victory is now familiar to everyone, though it was news in 1897. But even today, at the celebration of your Golden Jubilee, the contribution of the Irish American to our military history and our political history is better known than his role in education. We read how the Irish of a hundred years ago were laying the tracks of the Erie Railroad, as they had dug the Erie Canal, but we are vague on the process by which they pulled themselves up by their own bootstraps. Did you ever hear, for example, of Miss McKenna, the daughter of the McKenna of Tuam? Neither did I, until a few nights ago. She came to this country in the early 1840's, settled in Schenectady, at the time a rough frontier town where her countrymen were still covered by the mud of the canal. With sublime faith in the possibilities of even poverty-stricken Irish material, she opened up not a beginning, but a finishing school, where the ditch-diggers' daughters learned good French and music and painting and literature—learned them well, and became, in turn, teachers themselves. Later in life the remarkable Miss McKenna joined the Mercy Nuns and settled in Brooklyn, where as Mother Augustine she was a center of cultural influence until her death.

About the same time, the Right Rev. John Hughes, a grand, upstanding, fighting Irishman of a bishop, acquired the historic Rose Hill Manor, up in what was then Westchester, and began not only a college and a seminary, but a great movement, a movement to educate and raise to a new social level the Catholic immigrant of the Northeast, predominantly Irish, of course. At that time there was not a high school or a college or a seminary for Catholics north of Emmitsburg, Maryland, or east of the Alleghanies. It was Fordham—or what was then St. John's College—that lighted the way for all that were to come after. The present University was not, of course, the work of a single race, any more than of a single man. From the time when wigwams were pitched on the West Campus and our leading athletes were Tekamek, Rekowak and Pechinarius—sounds like a good backfield—various nationalities have mingled there in harmony to enrich the life of the institution. But since this is a private meeting, with no reporters present, we can admit among ourselves that from the time of its founder, who spoke with a touch of the County Tyrone, down to the present year, the little place has always been just Irish enough to be sure of herself. Her first President was Cardinal McCloskey; her first faculty included Ambrose Manahan, John J. Conway, Edward O'Neill and John Harley. Of course, there were a few names on the list that the old people would call "barbarius," like James Roosevelt Bayley—whoever heard of a name like that—but the tone in general was aristocratically Irish from the beginning. Of her twenty-five Presidents, four were French, two were English, one was German—and all the rest were just what they ought to be; the last fourteen, from the time of Father Dealy, being Irish without exception. It isn't that we are narrow about it, any more than you are, but everyone knows that of all varieties, an Irish Superior is the most docile, the most humble, the easiest to get along with—when he gets exactly what he wants.

However, this very quality that we joke about, this indomitable conviction of superiority, has been an important factor in sustaining Ireland through centuries of crushing persecution. In like manner, it has brought Fordham through many dark days of debt and misunderstanding. It has kept her convinced that hers is no ordinary destiny. In 1841 she opened her doors to hewers of wood and drawers of water, underprivileged exiles who were caricatured in all the intolerant papers of the time. She welcomed them and made them doctors and lawyers and teachers and writers, officers in the Army and Navy, priests and bishops—you could see the general level rising in every decade of years. And that story can be multiplied all over the country. But just as in the eighteenth century the Irish masters harvested one kind of crop in Ireland and another in the colonies, so in the 1840's were there certain differences. According to Padraic Colum—

> "You teach Greek verbs and Latin nouns,"
> The dreamer of Young Ireland said,
> "You do not hear the muffled call,
> The sword being forged, the far-off tread
> Of hosts to meet as Gael and Gall—
> What good to us your wisdom store,
> Your Latin verse, your Grecian lore?"

But the dreamer of young New York was eager for the culture that seemed pedantic to the struggling Irish.

Now the tide has turned again. The tradition of the liberal arts, "the Latin verse and the Grecian lore," is stronger in Ireland than it is in America. But the results are not what we might expect because of other complicating factors. Judging by 1776 and 1846, we should find internal unity and strong anti-British feeling on the other side with the liberal arts, and over here division and a moderate spirit of practicality and compromise. Actually, Ireland is still tragically divided by the garrisons in the north, and come July, Belfast will resound again with "Croppy, lie down."* (An American soldier, during the war, was amazed by the demonstration and asked what the shouting was all about. An Orangeman answered: "We are celebrating the Battle of the Boyne." "What," said the American, "was the Battle of the Boyne?" Speechless, the Orangeman could only gasp: "Read your Bible, man; read your Bible.") But in spite of the fact that everyone knows the stupid role Britain is playing in keeping open ancient wounds, and in spite of the recent memories of Lloyd George and his Black and Tans, the Irish are practical enough to realize that if England crashes, she will crash too, and no one in the world is waiting with deeper apprehension and more personal interest the threatened dismemberment of the British Empire and the bankruptcy of England itself than the citizens of Eire. It is only over here, where Ulstermen and Kerrymen can meet in friendship at a dinner like this, where we can compromise on everything else, that there is such zeal to avenge the crimes of Oliver Cromwell. The way some Irish Americans cheer at bad news from London, one would think that the Treaty of Limerick had been signed and broken yesterday; some have become enthusiastic Zionists and too many are opposing the President's stiff attitude toward international communism because they think it will save the British Empire. Let the Empire go. Let the term go, too—it is a nineteenth-century institution that has had its day. But the British Commonwealth of Nations is quite another thing. It is an essential element of the

* "Croppy," an orange term for Catholics derived from "sharecropping."

English-speaking world, of which the United States and Eire are other component parts. Anything that weakens the Commonwealth weakens us and Eire, too. Washington's vital interest in England's survival is not a sentimental, but a very practical one—as practical as Dublin's.

Let us hope, then, that your Society, in its next fifty golden years, following the trend now observable in Eire, will record the contributions of Irish Americans toward strengthening the union of the English-speaking world.

It Is Up to the Laity

The Catholic Club of New York, 1946

IT IS interesting that your Diamond Jubilee should come along just now, when people are taking a new interest in the place of the laity in the Church. It helps to emphasize the fact that we need the Catholic Club as much in 1946 as we did in 1871.

Of course the two dates suggest many interesting differences. In '71, for instance, it was a *Republican* President who did not know what it was all about, Ulysses S. Grant. At that time a European power was paying real money to the U.S. Government in settlement for the Alabama claims. Imagine our getting $15,500,000 from anybody! Chicken feed, I admit, but it is the sentiment of the thing! At that time the South was sending to the Senate Bilboes in reverse, carpetbaggers elected by the blacks to persecute the whites. Tremendous fortunes were being made, coal was being mined, and, Mr. Toastmaster, the Democrats were about to stage a comeback.

But there were similarities, too, as there always are in the history of a human nature that never really changes except through Grace. Paris was in the grip of a new force called Communism. From March till May of that year the Reds commanded the city and slew the Archbishop with scores of priests and religious. Rome had just fallen through cynical contempt for the sacredness of a treaty. The Holy Father was struggling with every shade of radicalism all over the continent and with a peculiar pagan statism in Prussia which was soon to come to a head in the *Kulturkampf*. The Vatican Council had just been adjourned *sine die* (not like the U.N., which is so often adjourned *sine deo*) and Bishop Oxnam's predecessors were all worked up over the separation of Church and State. Here in New York, St. Patrick's Cathedral was covered with scaffolding and a Fordham Archbishop (soon to become the first American Cardinal) directed operations.

It was therefore to Archbishop McCloskey, gentle, polished and amiable, that Father Patrick J. Dealy went with a Committee of his Alumni Sodality to explain the plan for the Xavier Union. Its object was to give the members of the Sodality a channel for their social and intellectual energy. The social aspect was to be a means of fostering a true Catholic spirit and of encouraging the study of Catholic history, literature, science and art. If in time the social aspect was to become something more than a means to these ends, it would prove merely that the Club was a human organization and needed an annual retreat. Personally, I should be the last to criticize a slight overemphasis on good fellowship with my own fond memories of many a New Year's Eve in the old ballroom on the second floor, with everyone linking arms at midnight to sing "Auld Lang Syne"! In any case, Cardinal McCloskey was farsighted enough to realize that he had here a picked group of intelligent Catholics filled with a spirit of devotion to the Church and fidelity to the Holy Father. So he took them under his special patronage—an example followed by all his most reverend and eminent successors.

The times just then were critical for the Church, even though '71 came in the lull between the defeat of Know-Nothingism and the rise of the American Protective Association. They were critical because our numbers were increasing rapidly without a proportional increase in public leadership. A generation before, we had been only a handful in New York and it was not surprising that so few Catholics stood out in the country. But by '71 there was a strong consciousness of disproportion on the part of thoughtful men. There were too many hewers of wood and drawers of water. Not that the Catholic Church ever was or ever will be ashamed of being the Church of the poor. That marks it as the Church of Christ. But it is, after all, supposed to be a Catholic Church, where kings and philosophers kneel beside the beggars at the Communion rail. All we needed in '71 were a few kings and philosophers. There were enough Catholic colleges in the area, but they were all small and struggling.

St. John's, at Fordham, would graduate six or eight a year, and Manhattan and Xavier about the same. St. John's in Brooklyn had just been founded. We hadn't a single professional school in the Northeast, and of course no graduate school or any appreciation of graduate work.

So Father Dealy, who was a man of culture as well as zeal and had great influence with the leaders of the city, non-Catholic as well as Catholic, devoted himself to giving the laity its place in the sun. With this end in view he did not confine himself to politics, though he did not despise them either. As a matter of record, he is credited with having made W. R. Grace Mayor of New York and unquestionably helped many others, but he was still more interested in the lasting leadership of the mind. He realized that if Catholic culture was to strike a taproot in American soil, we had to have laymen able to think for the unthinking masses; writers, literary giants—not merely journalists who would reach our own through Irish, German and diocesan papers—but men whose biographies, novels and plays would make a dent in public opinion (Newman's *Apologia* and *Grammar of Assent* had just appeared in England); we had to have scientists whose discoveries would be the strongest possible refutation of the calumny that science is the enemy of religion (Pasteur was then in his prime in the Sorbonne); philosophers who would penetrate the greatest lecture halls and libraries and at the same time walk the streets of the world and talk the language of the people, without ceasing to talk sense—men who could do for sound ethics and psychology what Huxley was doing for materialistic evolution, bring them into secular universities, into clubs, into lunchrooms; get the bankers and the horse-car conductors as familiar with the Natural Law and the spirituality of the soul as they were, in '71, with the missing link and the survival of the fittest. Nobody was doing that. All this, of course, was not to be directly produced by the Xavier Union. After all, its members would always be, in the main, business and professional men with families to support and little time for research and the writing of books. But they were to be the great source of encouragement and patronage. They were to be on the lookout for extraordinary Catholic talent and champion Catholic higher education.

How gratifying it would be at this, the Diamond Jubilee of Father Dealy's dream, to be able to say that it had fully lived up to his expectation, that the need for an intellectual lay apostolate was not as keen as it was in '71. As a matter of fact, however, it is keener—far keener. Some progress has been made. There are now at least two good Catholic graduate schools in the East and Catholic scholars are slowly beginning to multiply, but in proportion to the Philistines around us, we are still a pitiful handful, and of those whom we lean on most heavily too few are native-born Americans. We have wonderful lectures for the public, but too few come to hear them. What are we doing, as a group, for painting, sculpture, architecture and music, the children of Catholic tradition? It is true some of the clergy have sworn off buying marble altars out of a Sears, Roebuck catalogue, and as a result a few Catholic artists are able to eat—but only a corporal's guard of the laity has any interest in developing talent or even in helping a movement like the Liturgical Arts.

We need the Catholic Club. We need it terribly. Fine work is being done by the C. Y. O. and the Catholic units of the Boy Scouts and Girl Scouts of America. Zealous priests are keeping the Holy Name Societies together with good talks and round-table discussions on questions of the day, scaled to the average intelligence of their particular parishes. Labor schools are opening everywhere; there must be twenty in the Archdiocese by now. The K. of C. have an excellent educational program for the benefit of their members, and all these things are most admirable and most necessary.

But the leading Archdiocese of America cannot afford to stop here. It is, after all, the crossroads of the modern world, for which the Holy Father has shown his special predilection in appointing not only an extraordinary administrator who has balanced his books and has expanded every facility at the same time, but a literary figure whose sumptuous royalties are donated to charity, a world figure, the second best known priest in the Catholic Church.

This Archdiocese, therefore, above all others in America, deserves a large and zealous group of top-flight men selected not for their wealth or their title but for their intellectual and spiritual integrity; men who do not need lectures in the fundamentals of Catholic culture or practice—men who can give the lectures themselves; men who can understand the necessity of developing among the laity in the Church the highest flights of scholarship and of genius, who are willing to give their time, their enthusiasm, and—rich or poor—a proportionate amount of money, to develop Catholic scholars and artists. In other words, New York deserves the men whom Father Dealy had in mind when he founded the Catholic Club.

III

THE EDUCATIONAL PICTURE

The Age of Discretion

The Cardinal's Anniversary, May 4, 1964, The Waldorf Astoria, New York

TWENTY-FIVE silver years as a shepherd who can count one million seven hundred thousand sheep in his fold is something to celebrate, and with four thousand guests including sixty Cardinals, Archbishops and Bishops, even a Texan would admit that this is a celebration. But why all the excitement about seventy-five years? Every other man you meet these days is seventy-five and playing golf. Even an Eagle Scout wouldn't help a man *that* age across the street. After all, sixty is now the age of reason and seventy the age of discretion. So at seventy-five the average man is just beginning to think twice before he makes a fool of himself.

It is true that an occasional genius creates a sensation while he is still in the cradle. Michelangelo did his Pietà when he was a mere twenty-one. And names like Mozart, Shelley, Don John of Austria, and Alexander the Great may give the impression that only *young* blood counts. But as Al Smith used to say, let us look at the record.

Titian did *his* great Pietà at the reliable age of ninety-eight. Verdi wrote Falstaff at seventy-nine, and that opera is as gay as anything Mozart ever did. As for statesmen, Winston Churchill was no adolescent back in the forties when he was running things down in Washington. And to match Don John of Austria, give me Douglas MacArthur anytime. How old was Leo XIII when he startled the world with his *Rerum Novarum?* Eighty-one. And how old was good Pope John when he paused that day at St. Paul's Outside the Walls to tell a few Cardinals quite casually that he was going to summon an Ecumenical Council? Seventy-eight. Even Moses was eighty years of age when he began his great adventure in the desert, and I am not referring to Robert or the Flushing Meadow. Need we mention such energetic youngsters as Adenauer, De Valera, Salazar or Chiang Kai-shek, all good friends of His Eminence? We certainly don't have to mention General De Gaulle. He is perfectly able to mention himself. The ones we have to worry about these days are not the men of maturity but boy wonders like Fidel Castro and Malcolm X.

So where does all this historic round-up lead us? To the Waldorf and to the conclusion that when we wish His Eminence many happy returns tonight, this wish is possible of fulfillment. To us, he is a promising young man, so he has a future as well as a past, and a present, too, that in its own way is more interesting than either. These are the stirring times of the Aggiornamento and much of the responsibility for our understanding of ecumenism rests on the Cardinal's shoulders. For all the excitement, all the open windows involved and the long years of adjustment that are sure to follow, Catholic America is quite relaxed because the Holy Spirit has seen to it that there are enough Cardinal Spellmans among the Fathers of the Council. That is one reason why we are so confident that when the last session is over, there will still be Ten Commandments and Three Persons in one God.

Thus his future is rosy and his present inspiring, but his best friends cannot deny that he has a past, for His Eminence was not one of those late blooms that burst forth after being unknown in their early years. It is true that following his ordination the rate of his progress in Boston was, shall we say, moderate. Rome proved to be more appreciative. From the time when Monsignor Borgongini Duca singled him out for attention, he was a name and not just a number. At the early age of thirty-six, he had already made a favorable impression on the forthright Pius XI, and before he was forty, he was the most influential American priest in Rome. As a matter of fact, he was hovering on the outskirts of the Latern Treaty. Soon after that he found himself by the merest accident in Berlin as the guest of the Nuncio, a certain Monsignor Pacelli, and in a couple of months welcomed this future Pope to the Vatican State Department as the successor of Cardinal Gasparri. Providence continued to watch over the American Monsignor and three years later he was consecrated Bishop by the Cardinal Secretary of State.

As in the story of another Joseph, his seven years of plenty in Rome were followed by seven years in the Archdiocese of Boston, an admirable preparation in asceticism for what will be, we hope, many more than twenty-five years in the Archdiocese of New York.

By now he was approaching maturity. He was fifty years of age. What he has done with his twenty-five years, from fifty to seventy-five, is familiar to Your Excellencies of the American hierarchy and is written in the heart of every true New Yorker. Should we then enumerate the buildings he has erected, churches, schools, hospitals, homes, convents and rectories? Why, the cornerstones he has laid in twenty-five years would build an Egyptian pyramid. Should we analyze his miracles in real estate and finance involving sums that sound like the national deficit? Some other time you would find them fascinating, I am sure, but not tonight. The Waldorf has put us in too mellow a mood. Should we talk about his books then? Why not? Any man alive would be proud to have written eight books in ten years, everything from a prayer book to a full-blown novel. Any man would feel a glow if the total circulation ran well into seven figures and the royalties, all given to charity, established a record. But what sets the accomplishment apart forever in a class by itself is the fact that the author was at the time the busiest man in this mad, mad, mad city of ours. He was not only tending more than a million and a half sheep to everyone's satisfaction, especially the Holy Father's, but taking care of the White House, too. He was not exactly the President's spiritual father. Saint Franklin didn't need one of those. He had a direct line of communication. But this was his "favorite Bishop" and that took a lot of his time. History will record the extent of his services to his country, as well as to the Holy See, in the negotiations that preceded the appointment of Myron Taylor and on many other occasions as well. In Europe, the Italians have not forgotten the part he played in averting the destruction of Rome, and Hungarian Jews still remember what he did to save them from deportation. There were many busy days spent on War Relief, the Near East Relief, Catholic Welfare in the Philippines, the Catholic University and so on ad infinitum. Most of his time, however, in these critical years, was devoted to his favorite apostolate as Military Vicar of the Armed Forces.

He was with his boys in the thick of battle: flew into France when the Allies invaded from the South; into Germany just after the Siegfried Line was breached; entered Seoul in Korea on the day of surrender, and trudged on foot through miles and miles of American casualties, lying helpless and lonely in Army and Navy hospitals all over the world. One day, a young wounded soldier, unable to write himself, was trusting enough to think that the Archbishop of New York, covering all fronts with a program that filled every waking hour, would have plenty of time to drop the folks a line and say that Joe was doing all right. By one of those extraordinary coincidences, the Archbishop of New York happened to be just that kind of man. It is estimated that in the course of his wartime journeying he took the names of tens of thousands of Joes and had friendly letters sent to their folks back home, exhibiting in this a characteristic blend of charity and efficiency.

Some of us are just old-fashioned enough to find this more

impressive than any ceremony we have ever seen him engaged in, and that would include the Great Consistory of 1946, when we watched him as he received the red hat of a Cardinal with its wide brim and streaming tassels from the hand of his most exalted and dearest friend, Pope Pius XII, of such blessed memory. The world is interested mainly in his success that brought with it all the honors and decorations and degrees that are stored up over in the Chancery Office. What keeps his friends in the cheering section is not what he has accomplished but what he is. He is always the same, no matter whether he is talking to the greatest scientist in the country, a five-star General, or the boy who delivers the papers. No matter who is being entertained at lunch—and every respectable headliner in the world lands eventually at 452 Madison Avenue—their host is invariably an amiable and interesting priest with a sense of humor and a most disarming accent, a man who never tries to be impressive and never uses a pompous word except in jest. At the age of seventy-five, after twenty-five brilliant years in New York, he is still Mrs. Spellman's eldest son. You know, the one who studied in Rome. That doesn't mean that he is a simple character. He isn't. He is fearless, tireless and shrewd as any Yankee in Whitman, the wrong man to cross when he's right and you're not. But at the same time he is humble, whimsical, sentimental, incredibly thoughtful, supremely loyal, and above all, a real priest.

So tonight, after twenty-five eventful years, while we thank the dear Lord for all he has done for us New Yorkers through this illustrious and incurable Bostonian, we thank Him, too, that our Father in Christ is only seventy-five—still a promising young man.

Enough Breastbeating

Manhattan College Alumni Association, New York, 1958

ALUMNI dinners all over the country are meeting this week in an atmosphere of shaken confidence. Soviet success in the satellite field brought a rush of intemperate criticism and demands for radical changes in our higher education that would play havoc with some of the things we love as Americans. I am not referring to old-time sentiment and campus romanticism. You may remember the Princeton alumnus who shouted at Woodrow Wilson, "You have reduced my alma mater to an educational institution!" No, I am referring to essential values. These have been under fire.

To add to our uneasiness as alumni of a Catholic college, we are not allowed to forget a little spiritual sputnik of our own sent up by Monsignor John Tracy Ellis of Catholic University. He started a bitter controversy in family circles that is still going strong, and from the controversy has come the general conclusion, which was not his, of course, that bad as all American education may be, Catholic education is worse than the non-Catholic. Whatever scandal has been given or taken resulted not from his central thesis, but from the misunderstandings which followed his remarks.

In other words, his point was a good point, but by the time it got down to the market place it had been distorted into the impression that there were no decent Catholic colleges and universities in the country, so that now, up in the neighborhood of my little mission church on Park Avenue, we hear with increasing frequency from Catholics who have their heart set on St. Paul's and Yale, that according to leading Catholic educators there is no intellectual progress being made in Catholic institutions.

That, of course, was the last thing Monsignor Ellis had in mind when he read a paper entitled "American Catholics and the Intellectual Life" before a small group which calls itself "The Catholic Commission on Intellectual and Cultural Affairs." It was published afterwards in *Thought* and quoted freely in the secular and religious press of the country. Two years later, Father Gustave Weigel, S.J.,* who teaches ecclesiology in Woodstock College, read a somewhat similar paper before the same congenial group, "American Catholic Intellectualism —A Theologian's Reflections," and because of the previous flurry, the Catholic and secular press reprinted his learned if somewhat caustic and racy comments.

Thus far there was some licking of chops in the enemy camp; some said unctuously, "Thank God the Catholics are beginning to realize their limitations. They are beginning to realize how far they have to climb to reach our level." There was some escape of steam from underprivileged faculty members in struggling institutions. But, after all, the distinguished voices from two ivory towers did not immediately penetrate to the masses. It was not until Father John J. Cavanaugh of Notre Dame entered the lists in December last that everybody began to take sides. The latecomer who had been a successful athletic director before his elevation to the presidency, thought he was merely quoting the scholars and was astonished when he pulled the house down on his head. It seemed to some observers that the hierarchy and the Catholic press had taken the first two attacks with excessive humility and had already begun to feel a little bit annoyed with themselves, so that when the third reformer came along and rattled the same old family skeleton, they let him have it.

* Father Weigel died early in 1964.

Now what precisely were these friends of ours driving at? Monsignor Ellis wanted to prove that there are not enough Monsignor Ellises in the Catholic Church, and with that we are in full agreement. We could use many more such charming and learned prelates. He was talking about intellectuals and using "intellectual" in a very technical sense. "Intellectual" so used does not mean "intelligent." It does not mean "educated." It is used of a specialist, of one whose achievements are in abstract speculation, of a research man who publishes his conclusions in learned magazines. By way of illustration I might mention that in the fall of 1936 I invited Hilaire Belloc to come from England for the spring semester at Fordham and assigned him to the history department of the Graduate School. To my surprise some of the faculty members came to me and protested that their reputation would suffer because Hilaire Belloc was not an intellectual. He never used footnotes and, worse still, lectured in a way that mere bachelors of arts could understand.

In the same sense, of course, your Cardinal Mundelein was not an intellectual. The Chancellor of the University of the State of New York is not an intellectual. Brother Augustine Philip is no longer an intellectual. He was before he became president, but I prophesy that if he serves Manhattan as long as I served Fordham, he will have difficulty at the end spelling his own name on the diplomas, and the same is true of two Ivy League presidents I know who realize that their "intellectual" days are over.

But the point Monsignor Ellis wanted to make was that we have not produced our share of specialists. He charges, of course, that the whole United States is anti-intellectual, and quotes Merle Curti's witticism that "in the Old World an ordinary mortal on seeing a professor tipped his hat, while in America he tapped his head." But backward as the rest of the country may be, the Monsignor claims that Catholics are behind the rest of the United States. Unfortunately, his paper contains a number of *obiter dicta* which are a little difficult to establish and, more unfortunately still, a flash or two of personal annoyance. He quotes, for example, with some approval the vitriolic comment about Catholic education that was once made by Robert Hutchins in Chicago. This interesting and outspoken critic of all things human had been invited in a moment of aberration on the part of the officers to speak at the annual dinner of the National Catholic Education Association. To their embarrassment he gave the assembled delegates exactly what they deserved to get for asking him. He punched them right in the nose. What he said was that Catholic institutions had adopted all the worst features of secular education and ignored most of the good ones. It does seem a little sweeping, doesn't it? But accepting the charge in general, the Monsignor goes on to upbraid administrators, as usual, presidents, chancellors and deans. In that, he speaks for all the unappreciated faculty members in the country who gather each morning for their coffee break. Whenever they get together, they always come to the conclusion that *malum est in capite*—the trouble is at the top. Each one always says, "If our illiterate president would only have sense enough to stop collecting money and just concentrate on spending it for the research in my department, Old Siwash would be a real university." I know from experience that Brother Augustine Philip must have a feeling of deep sympathy with Rudolf Bing of the Metropolitan Opera Company. But all these interesting comments aside, the main point of the paper was that we have not got enough research men publishing in learned magazines.

Father Weigel had a somewhat different angle. He agreed with Monsignor Ellis that there was "an indisputable lack of Catholic intellectuals," and this he blamed largely on the way ecclesiastics are being trained in the United States. It was an interesting paper, with comments on seminaries that are seldom aired in public. Read at the annual Bishops' meeting down in

Catholic University, it would, of course, have been highly stimulating and I, for one, would have paid admission to be there. But quoted with relish in journals like *Time* and *Newsweek,* it gave the impression that we Catholics face a real crisis in intellectual inferiority.

When Father Cavanaugh's turn came, then, he thought that he was making the same shot, though he realized that he was putting just a little English on the ball. He said that "intellectual prestige of American Catholics is shockingly low" and cried out, "Where are the Catholic Oppenheimers—where are the Catholic Einsteins?" He could not have meant that just as it sounded, but in any case he ended by pointing the finger of blame at Catholic institutions. He pointed it, however, in a way that skirted despair. There was just a suggestion that amidst all this Catholic ignorance and decadence one beacon of hope was shining somewhere in the Middle West. One university was still worthy of financial assistance.

Now, what impression does this make on an innocent bystander, a Harry Truman of the educational world, who has time now to take a morning walk without reporters and philosophize?

Well, first of all, our critics seem to overlook the fact that two-thirds of our Catholic students are in non-Catholic colleges and universities. From this they should deduce that only one-third of them have an excuse for being handicapped, the rest ought to have had for some time now, a sporting chance to become Oppenheimers. (What a curious ambition!) If our coreligionists have not scaled such dizzy heights, we should either lay two-thirds of the blame on state institutions, the Ivy League and the Virginia Creeper League, or frankly admit that Nordics and Jews are more apt for research than Celts and Mediterraneans. That point granted, however, it seems to me that underneath all this hassle there is a foundation in fact. We do need more research men in every field. Sometimes the advances that are being made may seem trivial to an outsider. When you see a man, for example, who has been two full years on the back leg of one fruit fly, you are likely to say, "Is that worth twenty-four months of concentrated labor?" Perhaps it is. We cannot always recognize a little link in a very important chain. It may lead someday to a wonderful discovery. That is why we never belittle the curious subdivisions of a topic that are assigned to graduate students.

But the fact to be emphasized here and now is this: real progress in the field of research *is* being made already in many Catholic universities and if we know our history as we should, we are not impatient with the pace. To make that history concrete, let me be personal for a moment. One of my grandfathers was English and Protestant. He went to a good school, was accepted, and made money. The other grandfather was Irish and Catholic. He got what education he could from an old hedge master in the 1830's, and when he came to America lived his life out as a baggage master on the Erie. My father attended a little red schoolhouse in Port Jervis until 1866, and went to work in the roundhouse at the age of fifteen. My mother attended the best school Brooklyn could boast of in 1870, Packer Institute. When I was born, my eldest brother was a freshman at Yale, and intervening brothers tried out Brown, Columbia and Lafayette. By the time I graduated from high school, however, my father had learned enough about higher education to send me to Georgetown. This was still a small institution fifty years ago. There were 120 boys in the entire college, no graduate school of any kind, and a little medical school and a hospital, which, compared with what they have now, were holes in the wall. Since then, the pace at Georgetown has been reasonable, to say the least, and the same is true of Fordham, which I mention now only because my testimony happens to be firsthand. Twenty-five years ago Fordham had a graduate school, but it was making money and that is always a bad sign. It was located in the Woolworth Building, with part-time teachers and part-time students, and not a book on the shelves. The catalogue stated with disarming simplicity that the students had the use of all the modern facilities at Forty-second Street and Fifth Avenue. Just ten years later, due very largely to the work of my predecessor, the school was up on the campus, with full-time students and full-time faculty members, losing $110,000 a year, besides a lion's share of the $90,000 annual budget for the library. In 1936 four college seniors decided to go in for research. By 1956 the number was forty-eight, a percentage increase of from 2 per cent of the senior class to 16 per cent.

These are only personal statistics and local conditions, if you will, but characteristic enough to indicate the educational background and progress of most Catholics in the country. What I happen to know about Georgetown and Fordham, *mutatis mutandis* would be true of Manhattan—would be true of every important Catholic institution in America.

It might appear from this that our ultimate goal does not extend beyond the development of a campus swarming with intellectuals. It is true that the purpose of a university is to pursue truth, and for that we need research men. But that is not its only purpose. It must also teach the truth and guide society. In addition, therefore, to ivory towers, and I am not belittling ivory towers—there ought to be a few handsome ones on every campus—but in addition to the ivory towers we need classrooms, offices and chapels. If Monsignor Ellis were here, I would not dare say we also need gymnasiums. There I go—overemphasizing athletics again!

But all this means that we need good teachers, and a good teacher is very seldom a good research man, and a good research man is very seldom a good teacher. They are usually a different stripe of cat. Let it be said, too, in all modesty, that we need good administrators, administrators who are never research men, though sometimes ex-research men. Let us, then, be enthusiastic about research and everywhere give due honor to the publication of good books. But never let us fall into the sin of "bibliolatry."

It is possible, you know, to worship production and productivity for their own sake; to measure teachers exclusively by the number of books they produce. Where that is the case, an invaluable Mr. Chips could never expect a raise in salary, let alone a professorship. Too often in the typical American university we see the minimizing of the activity of a teacher in favor of research, a tendency which is traceable, of course, to the method peculiar to science and also to the naturalistic viewpoint that nature will yield ever new and valuable facts, and that new facts and the acquisition of new facts are more important than the preservation of wisdom and culture.

In addition, then, to a reasonable proportion of research men, we hope always to have our share of the few brilliant teachers in circulation. Some of them may have spent so much spare time with their students that they had no leisure to write for learned magazines, but their place with us will always be an honored one. We want our good administrators, too, men who can dream as well as beg, and be the lubricating element in the midst of specialists.

One more point and we are done for the night. We should like to insist, in closing, that we do not expect or desire the majority of our graduates to be intellectuals in the narrow sense. We need doctors, dentists, lawyers, engineers, parish priests, and all these we are training with increasing success. We need business men who will carry the principles of Christ into the market place and make them work. We need statesmen, too, who can survive the politics around them and rise to the top. But in answer to some of the statistics thrown at us in this controversy, we might add that we do not expect to live long enough to see rural America sending the graduates of Catholic colleges to Washington. To be President, a Catholic must still be an Ivy

League Catholic, and, when he goes to the White House, must keep an eye on the ministerial associations and not adorn his Cabinet or the Supreme Court with the graduates of places like Manhattan College. In short, we shall be satisfied to know that a reasonable proportion of our alumni are intellectuals, and a reasonable proportion leaders in nonscholarly fields. Both proportions we expect to be arrived at within a reasonable length of time. Be on your guard, then, gentlemen, against denunciations that ignore our minority position, our immigrant origins, our recent emergence, our racial characteristics, and all the other historical and sociological elements that have complicated the present situation.

Above all, when the acknowledged fact that our Catholic graduate schools are just emerging in the field of research is used again as evidence that we are failing to produce our share of well-educated clergy and laity, let the history of our many Manhattan Colleges throughout the land speak for all of us.

The Government, Religion and Education

The National Catholic Education Association, Philadelphia, 1949

IN THE fall of 1936, a distinguished visitor was welcomed by the Cardinal Archbishop of Philadelphia. The visitor was His Eminence Eugenio Cardinal Pacelli, Secretary of State to His Holiness, Pope Pius XI. With an admirable sense of fitness, the venerable host arranged that their picture should be taken standing before the Liberty Bell in Independence Hall, and with an instinct for public relations, no less admirable, the guest, as the picture was being snapped, placed his long, slender expressive hand above the surface of the familiar crack. Interpreted, the symbolism would say to the American people from the pages of the country's press, that the liberty for whose birth this bell was rung, the liberty of the Declaration of Independence, was not the liberty of the French Revolution, but the ancient liberty of Christendom; the liberty of the children of God. Moreover, the gesture would intimate that if in our times a crack has appeared in that great American ideal, it is not, like the crack in the bronze, irreparable. A damaged bell must be recast, but liberty can be made as good as new by the bare hand of man; in fact, by your hand and mine.

Apropos of all this, we are met to discuss in our convention "Relationships of Government, Religion and Education," a tremendous subject that proliferates before our eyes into a hundred subdivisions. For there are relationships between religion and government, and religion and education, and education and government, any one of which would keep the most reticent convention going for a week, and this is a convention of educators. It is, however, the prerogative of a dinner guest to select his own subdivision and his duty to keep an eye on his watch. So that, while we may refer obliquely to the purpose of education, the state of modern education, and the interminable row about the content of the curriculum, we shall do well to concentrate at this time on one phase of these multiple relationships, government planning, and examine its effect on religion and education. That is why we began by referring to the crack in the Liberty Bell.

In a dozen different ways, Washington is moving in on us. Some of its advances are inevitable and beneficent. We all admit, for example, that the laissez-faire independence of the nineteenth century robber barons had to go, and that in today's world some planning is most certainly a proper activity of the federal government, but the people should be made to realize that a point can be reached in over-all planning where they begin to surrender their essential liberties.

As Edmund Burke once said: "The people never give up their liberties but under some delusion." The Germans and the Russians and all the rest who have been planned out of existence were first deluded into thinking that liberty was a means and security the end—instead of just the other way around. And this has been one of the most fatal delusions of our times, times which may yet be known as the age of efficient chaos. For in practice this frantic scramble for security at any cost (and we are beginning to feel it now in education) has produced insecurity as the sole reward of all but a handful of tyrants. And yet, like a petty gambler who never learns his lesson, the common man is still playing with the temptation of staking liberty in a planned Utopia.

In this country, happily for us, a determined group seems to be emerging which realizes that something fundamental is in peril, and which refuses to stand by passively until "it has happened here." On such men, and it is encouraging to know that they are not by any means confined to the Republican Party, rests the responsibility for piercing the fog of delusion that surrounds too many of our fellow Americans, so that this nation's good sense, and inherent love of liberty, may vigorously reassert themselves.

The question of planning has been in the forefront for thirty years or more, though people still regard it as one of the picturesque distractions of the New Deal. During all that time planners and antiplanners, public enterprisers and private enterprisers, have tended to regard the issue as merely economic. They have ignored the more important moral and spiritual aspects of the question. The fact is that while this trend toward the over-all plan is usually studied in relation to the economics of trade, it is bound to influence every phase of human life influenced by economics. And to remind a group of school executives that every educational problem today bristles with economic implications is bringing, if not coals to Newcastle, certainly scrapple to Philadelphia.

Buildings, maintenance and school supplies are all reflecting the high cost of living. The nub of our problem, however, is the salaried teacher in the private college. He is becoming more expensive, more necessary and more difficult to find every year, largely for economic reasons that involve the government and affect the future existence of the liberal arts.

There was a time when a teacher's simple wants could be satisfied within the modest budget of a private school. A laborer was paid a dollar a day, and if the teacher got five, some sense of proportion remained. Since that bucolic era we have witnessed a mad race between wages and the cost of living in which the winner is still uncertain, but the odds are heavily on the cost of living. To meet the situation, farmers have been subsidized, workers have been mobilized, and every type of public benefit has been increased. When it comes to the teacher, however, a situation is developing where the unthinking private colleges are beginning to hope that the federal government will step in before they have to curtail their programs and sink to an inferior level. They realize that the problem will not be solved by giving the teacher a minimum wage commensurate with the cost of living index, though that may be more than they are giving him now. They realize that eventually they must go further than that. His compensation must be fixed with an eye to his relative dignity and relative importance in the community, or soon it will be impossible to persuade anyone with brains to teach. I know one institution which pays an electrician $5,200 a year, and this is as much as it pays an associate professor of physics. It pays the man who cuts the grass $2,000 a year, and this is almost as much as the starting salary of an instructor with a Master's degree. If the proper relations existed, the associate professor would be receiving from $10- to $15,000, and the young instructor not less than $5,000. Such a scale, however, in this particular but nameless institution, would increase the budget by $1½ million, so that in four years the debt would be almost hopeless.

Meanwhile, the salaried teacher is becoming more necessary every day. In two years our total Catholic student body has increased by 680,000 students. Our teaching priests and religious, whom I shall group together improperly as the clergy—for want of an omnibus title—have increased by only 3,800. Thus we have one new clerical teacher to every 180 new students. The lay teachers for the same period have increased by 3,000. May I remark, however, with a certain amount of emphasis, that while this fact adds to the financial problem of an administration, it is not to be regarded as a calamity. It is especially obvious in higher education that we need not only the infinite variety of training that only a group of laymen possesses, but we need the lay influence, and the lay viewpoint in our high schools, colleges and universities. As you realize so well, it is possible to overdo the clerical angle in education as in other fields. The clergy and the laity are supposed to complement each other in society as fathers and mothers do in normal families. The best man in the world cannot supply the touch that a woman should give in the home, and the best nun out of the world cannot prepare a girl for everything she is going to meet in life. I can think of many punishments which I should find more congenial than being condemned to a totally clerical society. Our lay faculties, then, are with us to stay, thank God—or are they?

Each year they become more difficult to find. This problem is linked in part with salaries. Only a man of independent means can afford to indulge his zeal for souls in the average Catholic school. Like a diplomat or an army officer, he has to have at least a rich wife. But linked with this is the deplorable policy in some of our more backward institutions of treating the lay teachers like rank outsiders and second-class citizens. Priests and religious, who are sometimes incompetent, are advanced over the heads of distinguished and experienced laymen, just because they are priests and religious, while questions of policy are seldom submitted to the honest comment of the whole faculty. That, I think, is one important reason why so many of our best Catholic scholars are seeking wider horizons. The main reason, however, is the enormous increase of opportunities for teachers in these days of educational inflation.

Washington seems to have set its paternal heart on having everybody over twenty dressed in a cap and gown—a generous impulse that may end by rocking the private colleges and universities to their foundations. Institutions able to reach into the federal pocket would establish a standard of extravagant operation which Princeton would find impossible to rival, and would inevitably wreck the faculties of colleges that depend on private support. It stands to reason that every good teacher with bills to pay would want to work for the government.

In dwelling on our fears, however, we run the risk of seeming to hold up progress for the sake of protecting vested interests. So let us say at once that we are thinking of the country's good when we think of our own. If the common weal demanded the death of private schools, private schools would have to go, but it is inconceivable that the common weal could ever demand it. Walter Lippmann has said somewhere that modern education is destined to destroy Western civilization by refusing to channel the religious and classical culture of the Western world—by deliberately neglecting the liberal arts. If we were to go a step further and select the most essential tradition of that culture, it would be the inherent dignity of man as a person, and that tradition has come to us not only through the family, the church and common law, but through the independent school. From this, no one should deduce that there is in any particular tax-supported institution a tendency toward the absolute state. But the school which is free from political pressure, the school where open-minded logical men can place a proper value on their spiritual heritage, is the independent school. Furthermore, it is significant that wherever absolute states have flourished, they have depended for their support on public, and therefore political control of all education. They have realized that here is a most important means for achieving that uniformity of ignorance which is essential for a Nazi or Soviet society. So that, without criticizing or even suspecting any particular college or university in the country, we can face the fact that the elimination of privately controlled institutions, or even their serious debility would remove a major obstacle from the path of a possible dictator in the United States.

And still, the federal government has legitimate relationships with education, and, up to a point, has a right to plan for it, just as it has a right to plan in the field of trade. In this latter field reasonable legislation which improves the quality of competition and provides a set of equitable rules within which economic activity might be carried out, is not only permissible, but highly desirable. The type of economic planning that strikes at liberty is not planning to make competition effective, but planning against competition. As someone has said, the government should seek to influence the economic weather, but not by trying to ration the raindrops. So too, with its relations to education, Washington can be helpful in many ways without interfering with the traditional rights of the individual states or the natural rights of parents. Without entering into disastrous competition with private education the federal government can influence the educational weather. For some federal assistance to private education, like some public assistance to any private enterprise, shows a grasp of changing positions in the world today. It is only federal control of private education, or worse, the smothering of private education by federal competition that would mark the beginning of the end. For all valuable differing points of view would thus be focused into one at Washington. With variety gone, choice would go with it, and liberty soon after. Moreover, without the tradition of the private schools to support them, the public schools would soon find themselves in the straitjacket of the absolute state where any education would be impossible.

So we stand today in salute before the Liberty Bell and, following the example of His Holiness, place our hand symbolically over the crack. What can we do here and now about the crack that is appearing in our educational liberty?

First, we can re-examine the administration of the institutions we possess and get our granaries ready, as Joseph did, for the seven lean years that are on the way. Let us ask ourselves a few direct questions. Have we been prudent, or have we allowed ourselves to splurge? Are we crushing ourselves, for example, under more architecture than we can carry? Fancy façades are like overemphasized athletics, a sure indication of the wrong-side-of-the-track mentality. The underprivileged always waste money on irrelevant display. Better one good plain school than two bad fancy ones. Better one well-staffed department than a dozen that would satisfy no one. Have we been charitable and loyal to our main objective, or have we engaged in stupid and expensive rivalries and duplications with other parishes, dioceses, and religious congregations? Have we been business-like in the way we run the treasurer's office, avoiding the smallest waste and budgeting a proper amount for replacement, before we begin to talk about profits? Have we been magnanimous in giving the salaried faculty the security and dignity which would keep them loyal to Catholic education, even though they could do better elsewhere?

By this type of self-examination we can go far toward insuring our survival in the transition period that faces us, but this will not be enough unless at the same time the public is aroused to the danger of too much concentration in Washington. We can be sure that the Most Reverend Bishops through their pastors will exercise the teaching power of the Church. The Catholic parents of this country will be warned through the press and the pulpit that their interest in education should not be confined to the parish. They will be made to realize that they are citizens of the United States concerned with everything that happens in all the schools which benefit from their taxes, and especially concerned with any type of educational planning on the part of the federal government that may infringe on their God-given liberties.

Colleges in the Market Place

Honors Day at Brooklyn College, New York, 1955

IT IS now a bare twenty years, one skimpy generation, since this beautiful campus began to emerge from a real estate development. Brooklyn College when I knew it first was hardly more than educational prime matter, with various trends and theories still battling for the right to give it its permanent form. On one side, there was a band of progressives and measurers determined to perpetuate the revelation of Morningside Heights, and on the other, a group of grim traditionalists carrying the banner of the Liberal Arts and shouting the slogans of Norman Foerster. Everyone knew that the principal aim of the new institution was to help with the education of our teeming millions in the secondary and grade schools, but was it to be a college of methods or a college of content? Would the emphasis be on "how" or on "what?" Was the faculty to be preoccupied with skills or with an inner fire?

Nothing had been settled with finality when I came over one day to represent my University at the inauguration of your second President.* He was known as a distinguished young economic liberal, fresh from Morningside Heights. That raised the hopes of some, especially when they heard that he had crossed swords in Chicago with bright young Thomas Aquinas Hutchins. Those of us, however, who were frankly biased in the oppo-

* Dr. Harry D. Gideonse.

site direction found comfort in the fact that he was Dutch. We were sure that no one educated in Holland or in any respectable part of Europe could underestimate the Liberal Arts, and we were right. Largely through his influence in preserving and developing the fondest dreams of his predecessor, the intervening years, some of them stormy and some of them bitter, have seen Brooklyn molded into a college of content where it is recognized that the Liberal Arts are an essential ingredient of modern life, especially the life of a modern teacher.

The soundness of this viewpoint has been lately confirmed from an unexpected direction, from the market place, from the world of business. Of course, the implications are not the same for you, the pampered children of Father Knickerbocker by his second wife, as they would be for a struggling private institution like Columbia. Poor Doctor Butler was always in critical need of another twelve million dollars and never went out to a dinner or even a football game without a tin cup in his pocket. All your fortunate President has to do when he wants another million is to phone the request to an indulgent board. But the new attitude of the market place toward literature, history and philosophy is a phenomenon worthy of study even in municipal circles where you are independent of private benefactions. It shows how new needs in the world around us can change the extension of the term "utility."

A few years ago "utility" would have been an offensive word to use in connection with a College of Liberal Arts. Its faculty would have insisted that its purpose was not utility; it was to teach the young how to live; not how to make a living. What they said really came down to this: "Let the students go to some grimy professional school to learn how to get ahead in the world or to some equally grimy graduate school to count semicolons in the First Folio with an eye to a Doctor's hood and a higher salary. We teach them through the Liberal Arts how to use their leisure hours, how to appreciate beauty in every form, especially the form of verbal expression. We have nothing in common with the world of business." And the business world promptly answered: "You're right! We shall therefore give our money to the things that interest us, to the technical preparation of experts, to practical projects of public health or to further research in the field that concerns us most."

After the First World War, however, the increasing importance of economics, political history and the physical sciences as components of the Liberal Arts course began to give the colleges some claim to the attention of the market place, so that the emphasis in many colleges underwent a noticeable change. The air was soon full of pre-medical, pre-law and pre-engineering. A curious degree appeared on the scene: a B.A. in B. A.—a Bachelor of Arts in Business Administration. The Liberal Arts of tradition was beginning to sink beneath the waves of a practical sea. An Oxford don, Isaiah Berlin, when he returned home about this time after an exchange professorship at Harvard, had this to say of the students he met here: "Many of these excellent young people could not even read or write as these activities are understood in our best universities; could not, that is, order, connect and discriminate."

Then came the thirties with their sudden spurt of Neo-Humanism. Scholars flocked to a standard that would lead them against Scientism, Naturalism and Progressivism, a standard that was kept occasionally at least in the armory of the University of Chicago. There they had a President* at the time who was as modest as he was taciturn, but a man with the courage of his convictions, which were numerous. He believed that a university could have a great President or great football, but not both, so instead of resigning he dropped football. With the aid of Mortimer Adler, the discoverer of St. Augustine and other obscure Fathers and Doctors of the Church, who was known locally

* Robert Maynard Hutchins.

as the Jew who was making Catholics out of Protestants, he evolved the Great Books program and fought violently with large sections of the faculty. They called him, appropriately enough, the Great Bookie. The Bachelor of Arts degree he threw into Lake Michigan on the charge that it was "the protector of an archaic and disintegrating collegiate organization, given at the wrong point for the wrong reasons." But the height of his idealism and courage was attained when he turned thumbs down on honorary degrees for mere industrialists. In this beau geste too many followed his example and the financial ice age descended again on the Liberal Arts. Up to and including the first year of the Second World War, the curricular trend in the colleges was encouraging enough, finding its most publicized expression in the Harvard and Yale Reports, both of them recognized as echoes of the *Ratio Studiorum*. But with all this progress made in reinstating the Liberal Arts, there was growing anxiety with regard to their support. If a professor of literature was to receive as much as a member of the Typesetters Union, the college would have to get the money from the federal government, a prospect that made private institutions fear for their independence.

Then suddenly, almost without warning, the sky began to brighten. The colleges saw a new way out of this dark dilemma. It was no longer to be "hell or Connaught," extinction or federal aid. There was now a *tertium quid* in sight—Big Business. This time, however, it was not the Liberal Arts that had changed, but the men in the market place. Great corporations, schooled in world trends, and now thoroughly frightened by what they had seen, began to extend the word "useful" until it covered not only the things of the counting room but even the things of the spirit. As a result, an increasing number of gifts have been announced, some like Henry Ford's $250 million for teachers' salaries, that are aimed exclusively at the preservation of the Liberal Arts, while others like the Sears, Roebuck and

Time-Life benefactions, by making scholarships available in any college of the winner's choice, are aimed in the vast majority of cases at benefiting the cause. Similar appropriations are now confidently expected from enlightened labor unions as well as from the stockholders of oil and automobiles, for all the responsible businessmen in the ranks of labor and management seem more than ever to have something in common. They seem to be going conservative in the best sense of that much abused word.

There was a time when big business was too often identified with wild speculation, and the unions with disorder. It was so in the days of the Fisks and Goulds and Vanderbilts and even later when Morgan and Hill and Harriman held the spotlight while the country held its breath. These old-timers rocked the United States Treasury with their battles for the Erie Railroad and the Knickerbocker Trust, but today big men are fighting for very much higher stakes without rocking anything in Washington. Responsible labor leaders and financiers are beginning to fight for the preservation of our way of life. And this they are doing not only because they are, in private life, fathers of families, citizens of their country and creatures of Almighty God who can see in a worldwide threat to our Western inheritance, a threat to their homes, their country and their religion, but because as businessmen guided by the profit motive they need our way of life; they need peace and freedom and integrity and above all, perhaps, hope. Despair, the spirit of modern culture, is bad for business as it is for everything else.

No one, however, should blame the directors of a great corporation for not recognizing sooner the importance of the Liberal Arts. These have been, after all, dark and bitter years since our World War began in 1914, years marked by so much disaster, so much destruction of wealth, beauty, life, health, purity, justice and charity that the fate of the Liberal Arts might well have seemed to such men a very minor tragedy until they began to realize that a great part of the surrounding gloom was due to the absence of intellectual as well as spiritual light. You remember the famous speech made by Viviani in the Chambre des Deputés a half-century ago when he felt that he had annihilated religion in France: "This day," he cried, "we have put the lights out of heaven and they will not be rekindled in our time." It has been left to our day to see the lights of secular learning going out all over the world. On the mainland of Asia, the darkness is impenetrable, but the twilight in Europe is even more alarming. Europe, after all, has been for two thousand years the source of Western culture—Judean and Greek culture baptized in Eternal Rome—and the universities have been for centuries the storehouses of Europe's thinking. Russia and Germany were casualties before the war, Italy to a less degree. In all of them, the discovery and transmission of truth, the creation and appreciation of beauty, had been distorted to further political ends. After the invasion of Poland, the Liberal Arts died out in a dozen other foreign countries, a brutal fact underlined by the opening of the Free University in Exile at Strasburg. There, one hundred and twenty-five refugees have gathered as the pitiful representatives of the whole slave world to study not methods of manufacture but philosophy and history and their own native literature. In Western Europe, where universities are still bravely rebuilding after the storm, the planners are plagued not so much by poverty as by the dread of invasion and war. But even if their fears prove to be groundless, even if the strange, fat smile in Moscow turns out to be something more than a sardonic grin, how many generations will it take to restore what Europe used to regard as ordinary? Conservationists are worried in this country because four inches of topsoil which were thousands of years accumulating have been washed away since the Declaration of Independence. The culture of Europe has lost more than four inches of its topsoil, and when will that be replaced?

This is the sobering loss which our great corporations have to contemplate. It is a loss that finds no compensation whatever in the breathless pace of our scientific discovery. As Charles A. Lindbergh has written so movingly in *The Spirit of St. Louis:* "I saw the science I worshiped and the aircraft I loved, destroying the civilization I expected them to serve, and which I thought as permanent as the earth itself. Now I understand that spiritual truth is more essential to a nation than the mortar in its cities' walls." With the same reasoning, our industrial leaders have come to the conclusion that for the next few decades at least, preservation is even more important that further advancement. That is why thoughtful men today are conservative men, in the original meaning of *conservare*. They want "to gather together and preserve" the inherited treasures of our past which we call civilization, and study has convinced them that these treasures have come to us through four main channels of communication: the family, the church, the courts of law and the Liberal Arts. The inner life of a family is beyond the reach of a corporation. The church means too many things to too many people to be the object of corporate giving, and the courts of law must be regulated from within and publicly supported. But the Liberal Arts can be directly subsidized, protected and developed, so that when in the future we see General Motors or Standard Oil, or the International Ladies Garment Workers Union giving millions for the preservation of the Liberal Arts as a channel of tradition, we can attribute their motive not to sentimentality, but to sound business sense.

A New University in Our Midst

Long Island University, New York, 1954

THE congratulations we offer President Connally this evening come straight from the heart. They are offered to an educator and a sailor who faces no ordinary humdrum campus job, but the exhilaration of a challenge—a challenge to develop a practically new University in the City of New York. It is pleasant to celebrate a bicentennial, but for real stimulation give me a new institution where a man can make the traditions and watch them grow, especially in New York.

Living as we do in an atmosphere of light and life with the glories of Long Island so easily available—within sight of Greenpoint!—it is hard to realize that honest folk in the great beyond, that is, beyond the Hudson River, know so little about God's country. They are almost as benighted as Europeans.

Cycling one summer in England near King's Lynn, I stopped to talk with two little country lads sitting on a stile. "Whar ye frum?" they asked me. "From far away," said I. "Frum Yarmouth?" "Farther than that." "London?" "Farther than London." Then, preening unconsciously like a Romano di Roma touring in Calabria, I added, "My home is in New York."

They looked at one another and closed the subject saying, "We never 'eared on it."

I naturally inferred that they had never heard of the United States either, because in many parts of Europe the United States and New York are coterminous—just as they are in New York. That, of course, is a harmless vanity to which outsiders gradually accustom themselves when they begin to feel as we do about the two chief sources of our complacency. The first is the natural beauty of the Empire State. From Lake George to Niagara, from the St. Lawrence to the Palisades, there is a variety of appeal difficult if not impossible to match elsewhere. The second is the group of colleges and universities—state, municipal and private—that have been growing organically in every part of the state for two hundred years, until today it can be said that New York shares with Pennsylvania a unique position of leadership in the education of the country.

A subject of pride at any time, just now the situation seems positively providential. Here we are the principal gateway through which Europe pours into the United States—pours in with all its color, its cultures and its contagious diseases. Certain of these diseases can elude the utmost vigilance of quarantine: political diseases, curious ideological diseases. Of these, the most dangerous by far at the present time, we call totalitarianism. It is a mental sickness that makes men turn to an absolute state, red or black, for the regulation of their destiny. In times of confusion, it promises order—the order of death, but order. In times of exhaustion, it leaves decisions to somebody else—even little decisions on what a man may wear and what he may eat and, most horrifying of all, what he may laugh at.

As a temporary condition, this can be brought about by a pampered army and a secret police, but such slavery to endure must be the result of slanted education. This control may be violent and corroding as it was in Nazi Germany and still is in the Soviet world where the single aim has been for years the closing of the human mind, or it may be gentle and insidious, as it was in Fascist Italy before the fatal Axis was formed. In 1927 when the whole thing was a novelty, I spent the summer in a Fascist university, the Regia Universitá Italiana per Stranieri da Perugia. We had a distinguished faculty drawn from a dozen ancient seats of learning and assigned there by the government to impress us foreigners with the splendor of the Duce's achievements. The lectures that year were on the seventeenth century, its history, its economics, its art, its music, its letters. But running through them all was the unmistakable implication that Italianità to be glorious must be controlled—government-controlled. That year the future of Italy was far from determined. All she needed to preserve the obvious material gains she had made, and her freedom as well, was a system of independent higher education. If, instead of a string of government-supported, government-controlled, government-enslaved universities she could have relied upon the scores of free and independent institutions that are the pride of our sovereign state, Italy could have had discipline without chains, glory without guilt.

In America we are more fortunate. Even our public institutions are not shackled. Their students and faculties are thoroughly, sometimes boisterously, democratic. They criticize the government as freely as their private neighbors do. This is especially true of the splendid municipal colleges in the City of New York. There have even been times when we had a fifth column in our educational world without going under. A few years ago we had a whole crop of starry-eyed liberals, some of them university residents, who could not distinguish between the human inconsistencies of a democracy like ours and the barbarities of our sometime gallant ally. Reinhold Niebuhr was thought rather bold when he nailed their attitudes as "sheer moral perversity," but he went on to say, "If we cannot make a distinction here, there are no historical distinctions that have any value." Since then we have seen the great disillusionment. Vodka has practically vanished from faculty clubs. Gin is back. Some maladjusted intellectuals may have gone underground for the duration, but since the duration will probably last another ten years, they will be harmless old Rip Van Winkles when they emerge.

It is one of the glories of our new alma mater, Long Island University, that its faculty has never given cause for the slightest suspicion of disloyalty. But even the condition that existed in some other and older institutions, alarming as it was, could still be corrected but only because the absolute state is not entrenched in City Hall or in Albany or in Washington. If it were, the power of appointment and the power of subsidy could soon lay down the party line to a public university, especially if it had not the moral support of numerous and influential private institutions. We can be grateful then, as Americans, that Europe's main impact on the United States today is here in New York where many generations of enlightened Americanism are at work to neutralize the poison of the absolute state.

All this applies in a particular way to the universities in the City of New York. Strictly speaking, there are only five of us, but in a wide sense that takes in all the various fields of higher education, we are a large and very interesting family of stepbrothers. In the first group, which we might describe as the children of Father Knickerbocker by his first wife, we count five privately owned universities; three on this side of the Tiber, Columbia, N.Y.U. and Fordham, two across the river in what is locally described as "God's Own Country," Long Island University and St. John's. This modest little group of five is keeping very quiet and behaving itself in the confident hope it will manage to survive somehow in this difficult world, living meanwhile on the crumbs it can gather for its daily bread from these $100-a-plate dinners. I know that Doctor Kirk is in distressing need of another thirty million, and we in L.I.U. could certainly use a dollar-and-a-half ourselves. The second group, which might be described as the children of Father Knickerbocker's second wife, consists of four flourishing municipal colleges which have cream in their coffee and gravy on their potatoes at every meal. The third group is made up of a surprisingly large number of private colleges and professional schools. While the greatest variety exists among them and marked individuality, they are all urban in both senses of the word; in the more general sense of being situated in a city and the more particular sense of catering in great measure to city students who intend to live their future lives in the city. This does not mean, of course, that we are not national institutions as well, but merely that what we have in common and what we treasure is our natural urbanity, a quality that springs from our maturity, our traditions, our strength, and our sense of the practical. We are strong because we never have to worry about registration and consequently never have to lower our ideals. Like everybody else, we are begging for bequests and endowments, but most of us have all the tuition we can handle. We are mature and practical because we are in constant contact with the beating heart of today. That may sound terribly modern and yet it is just what my Father, Ignatius Loyola, would have said in 1540. A couple of old Latin hexameters used to describe the difference between Ignatius and the other founders of great Religious Orders:

> "*Vales Bernardus, Benedictus colles amavit,*
> *Oppida Franciscus, magnas Ignatius urbes.*"

The others loved the valleys, the hills and the little towns, but Ignatius loved the great big cities as we do. Remote cloisters in the green hills have their charm and our nostalgia for them in after years can be keen. If I had my undergraduate days to live again, I should probably weaken and look for a cloister in the hills, but that is because there is something the matter with me. I go so far as to prefer Cambridge to Oxford.

But no matter what I should do myself, I should certainly advise a young man about to enter college to choose a conservative institution in a great city where he can hope to keep a good grip on the past, but live in the present and plan for the future. And this holds particularly true for a student in the City of New York. Oh, I know it is not the place it was when I was a little boy and Senator Wagner was studying in Law School, but still, as a city, it is greater than it ever was in the days of its charm. It is a city that for generations to come will probably control the world. Americans west of the Hudson hate to admit it, but they come to New York as a Gascon goes to Paris. Europeans are loath to admit it, but they come to New York as a farmer goes to the market. South Americans are the only ones that are frank about it. They call it the capital of the New World, and it is. But why stop at the New World? It is in fact the capital of the whole Free World. Let us see for a moment what that means for Long Island University. It means that L.I.U. is in the center of ideas, where, more than anywhere else, Europe and America come to focus. Word has gone the rounds that New York is the place where things are going to happen and the best minds in academic circles want to be here. It means that L.I.U. is in the center of population where we shall never have to wonder where our student body is coming from, where all we have to do is to achieve excellence and then choose the best. It means that L.I.U. is the center of wealth where we can most readily collect the sinews of war. The other institutions in the East all place their financial hopes in New York, but fortunately for us, their extracting power is inversely as the distance. When New York is fully conscious of what L.I.U. is planning to do and what we are doing, the city will be solidly behind us. I do not mean merely the devoted alumni who in a new institution like ours are young and impecunious. I mean every hardheaded businessman who has the real interests of New York at heart. We happen to be one of the safety spots around here, and thinking people are beginning to notice it. It means finally that L.I.U. is in the center of publicity. New York is the sounding board of the nation and everything here from restaurants to universities becomes a part of the national life. New York is the radio capital of America. New York news has the first call on all the great news syndicates and the New York papers are national papers. Nobody reads the Washington *Star* north of Chevy Chase. How many here, for instance, can remember two articles in the last year on Vanderbilt University or Duke, both very rich institutions? Yet the influential people of North Carolina and Tennessee read about Long Island University every time it makes a headline. They have to, if they read the New York papers.

Faced with such an opportunity, L.I.U. must brace itself to resist an obvious temptation—overexpansion. Its registration should always be determined by the supply of truly competent teachers who can devote themselves to really educable students. If it clings to that ideal, it will always remain a small university but a good one. The day it loses sight of that ideal and thinks of success in terms of numbers, it will sink to the level of a business enterprise. We must always be select, but not in any snobbish sense. Financial or social position will never harm or help a student in L.I.U. We need to be on our guard, however, against the loose terms "democracy of education" and "equality of opportunity." All around us we find the supposition that in a democracy everyone is entitled to not only as much education as he can absorb, but as much as he may for any reason desire. The result has been that too many American benches are filled with young people who have neither the interest in nor the capacity for advancement. It has been a normal condition of American colleges for years that one-third of the so-called students were in the way, cluttering up the place and interfering with other people's intellectual progress. If we need more room to take care of the expected population boom in 1960, let us create a good part of it by clearing out the useless lumber that we have already on our campuses. That will be like adding one new institution to every two in existence. If we were to find an adequate teaching staff for the 2,150,000 students that we have at present, we should have to comb the entire earth. We could not find them in America. Real teachers are not born every day. Bernard Giddings Bell, who has an unusual record for bull's-eyes, said recently, "The teacher has not fallen down on the job; the job has fallen down on the teacher." He is right. The job expected of the American teacher is crushing him, and that is largely the fault of the American public. If we could confine our efforts to the educable, we might find enough good teachers to educate them. But the proper screening of students is a principle which the American public finds difficult to accept. It is not supposed to be democratic. A year or so ago, Elmo Roper asked me to serve on an advisory committee to sample opinion in the United States with regard to higher education. The results of his poll were rather depressing to a student of Americana. It revealed that 83 per cent of our fellow citizens wanted their sons in college and about 69 per cent wanted their daughters to have the same advantage. But only 3 per cent cared whether or not their children were of college material. They regarded advanced study as a kind of tribal initiation with no intellectual implications. This is a situation for which I can offer no immediate solution except to suggest that we appoint another Senate Investigating Committee.

It is true that we are launching tonight a program of expansion. But what we seek involves no watering of our intellectual stock. Under the leadership of a distinguished educator whose ideals of a learning man are as high as his ideals of a fighting man, we are asking only for the expansion of those facilities that are necessary if the excellent students we have are to meet successfully the tremendous challenge of New York.

IV

A LITTLE IRISH PREJUDICE

The Green above the Red Left

The Friendly Sons of St. Patrick, Los Angeles, 1953

TWELVE years ago I had never been to California. That was the skeleton in my closet. My secret shame. Having spent my life in a modest seaport town on the Atlantic Coast, where the only point of interest was the birthplace of Cardinal McIntyre, I was still so backward that I thought San Francisco was in a class with Los Angeles. Then out of the blue came the first invitation to address this distinguished group on the Seventeenth of March. Unfortunately, however, the Japanese—who cannot even now tell a good Irishman from an Orangeman—picked that particular time to appear on the horizon in submarines, and the gallant sons of St. Patrick retired to the Mojave Desert. So that year I remained in New York and attended the counterpart of your celebration at the Astor. Seated at the head table, near Archbishop Spellman, was his new auxiliary whom I had known, incidentally, as a young Wall Street tycoon just making up his mind to enter the seminary. We were all prepared even then to see him go far—though not quite this far! Some thought it would be Newark and that would have been excellent. But Cardinal Archbishop of the Angels! That is eminent indeed. Our dinner was a success, and Al Smith wound up the evening with a blast at a White House which he did not consider as white as it might be. All around us that night red plans were moving on schedule, and except for a brief interlude at the time of the Hitler-Stalin Pact, the Soviet agents managed to create for the next ten years a state of national fog in which all kinds of reds and pinks and starry-eyed dreamers became an amorphous mass of Communist Fronts with the most alarming influence.

Tonight, with all eyes turned on Moscow, we have St. Patrick's permission to overcome the usual reticence that surrounds our pride of race, and admit in public, even in the gracious city where Gurley Flynn was so recently on trial, that almost no Irish names have graced the lists of those who were betraying their country through all these years. Furthermore, it can be said that of all the countries in Europe today no one has proved less fertile ground for the Kremlin than Innisfail—the Isle of Destiny.

The explanation is not, of course, that we shrink from a good revolution. We never did that. It was said in the English Parliament that fifty per cent of Washington's army was Irish. Actually it was only thirty-eight per cent, but the redcoats for some reason seemed to think it was more. Certain it is that at Valley Forge on St. Patrick's Day the Father of his Country ordered all his troops, even those unfortunate enough to be foreigners like himself, to drink a great toast to the Dear Dark Head—in fact one toast for every snake that had been driven out of her. From that day there wasn't a laggard in the American army. The Yankees and the Pennsylvania Dutch marched out of Valley Forge singing "O'Donnell Abu" and did their bit to help the Irish win the war. A year before that, thirteen Irishmen had signed the Declaration of Independence, and you can see from their penmanship the joy they took in the trouble they were making. Most of them, it is true, were left-footers, but I'll say this for the left-footers (under the hypnotic influence of the evening): their theology may have played hob with their sense of humor, but it never dimmed their Irish courage or their passion for independence. Yes, we relish a revolution, but it has to be a good one. We have no time for anything like the one they had in France, which was fought to destroy tradition. We liked the one in the thirteen colonies, which was fought to preserve tradition; and come the red revolution here, the Irish in Los Angeles will greet it with a song in their hearts.

It is not therefore the violent aspect of communism that repels us, neither is it the ancient ideal of sharing with the neighbor. Public ownership of the means of production and equal distribution of wealth, while posing many economic and moral problems, would have their attraction for any people crushed so long under a bitter and degrading poverty. Of course, it wasn't as if we were lower-class. The poorest of us could always look back to a time of power and affluence—somewhat distant—but very vivid. It was well known along the Shannon that when the barbarians in Britain were living on acorns, the people of Roscommon all had the gout. An Irish proletariat is a contradiction in terms, but we did go through a temporary financial embarrassment that lasted from the Danish Invasion to the Easter Rebellion and through most of those eleven hundred years philosophical communism must have had a strong attraction for our fathers. In fact, a Jesuit from Limerick named Thomas Field was one of the leaders in the most successful experiment ever made in philosophical communism, the so-called Reductions of Paraguay.

Finally it should be stressed that an Irishman's natural aversion to communism in its present form, which happens to be the product of a Russian and a German Jew, cannot be attributed to any aversion whatever to Germans, Jews or Russians. Just look around tonight. You will see all three at the next table, perfectly at home and as welcome as the spring. The Germans may be like their English cousins at times—a little bit on the practical side—but some Jews and Russians are enough like us to be German cousins. I used to think when the wonderful Goldbergs were on television that if Molly had a nice brogue and a slightly different profile, she could often have doubled for Mother Machree. The unspoiled Russians are even more like the Irish. Their deep faith, their melancholy and their sudden laughter, their incurable romanticism and their interminable arguments that never get anywhere, are very much like our own. There are a few differences, of course. They are simple, and our worst enemies never called us that. They are slow-witted and easy to push around, and tend to look for suffering and to wallow in it. But these are differences that make it all the easier for an Irishman to handle them, and we are famous for getting along with people we can handle.

Unfortunately, however, these are not the qualities reflected by the authors of the only form of communism known to us today: Lenin's interpretation of Karl Marx. What we have about us in America is a distillation of the worse traits of Germans, Jews and Russians injected into the veins of so-called intellectuals that it may break out later in a political rash. What they have in Malenkov's Russia is even worse, because unrestrained by any democratic tradition. There it is a stark and cynical tyranny all too familiar to be attractive. The Irish, like the Poles, have nothing to learn about purges and state-made famines. They went through the relocation of populations when Connaught was their Siberia and later the Barbados and Bounty Bay. The landlords taught them all about collectivism as well as ruthlessness, and as for official liquidation, there are men sitting with us here tonight who have seen their relatives and friends routed out of bed by OGPU's dressed in black and tan. You can fool an Irishman in many ways if you know him well enough. You can play on his vanity, his superstition or his prodigality, but tyranny you cannot sell him under any guise—unless of course you promise to let him be the tyrant.

Then what about George Bernard Shaw—publicist, playwright, philosopher and faker extraordinary? Didn't he say that the Soviets had the only civilized government in the world, and wasn't he a great Irishman? Not too much of a one. He brazenly admitted having a trace of Oliver Cromwell in his veins and that must have addled the rest of his blood. It was a species of diabolical possession. But he was Irish enough to have a strong sense of superiority—a pleasant weakness that never has to be rooted in fact—and a Gaelic talent for saying enraging things in an engaging manner. Moreover, he was as witty as a Dublin cabby, and though he had no religious scruples to bother him, shrewd enough to see through the bloody farce in Moscow. For all the silly compliments he paid them, they never could get him to settle down in the Communist paradise, because he knew that his popularity was linked to his irreverence and that if he made one irreverent remark about Uncle Joe, the Shavians at home could start preparing his niche in Westminster Abbey.

Aside from the sordid frightfulness of the Soviet government, however, even the academic theories of Moscow could never appeal to an Irishman. Take for example this wild idea of absolute equality played up in the Soviet press. The Russians do not mean the spiritual equality of the Declaration of Independence and the American Constitution, an equality based on the fact that all men are persons, individuals, that is, with spiritual faculties and a spiritual destiny so overpoweringly great that it dwarfs all differences. No. They mean an obviously false absolute equality that came down from the Stoics through the mad men of the French Revolution. No Irishman has to be told that men were never equal physically, intellectually, morally or socially and never will be. Even among the pagan Celts everybody had an immediate inferior—a fact from which no one ever deduced that everybody also had a superior. St. Patrick, who set up 365 churches before he died, knew his people well enough to consecrate 365 bishops. But time marches on. There is not a bishop left in Ireland now. They are all popes.

Another theory that would get a cold reception in Irish circles is the necessity for blind obedience to the Party, especially when it is the Republican Party. That is so hard for the children of Kings, and who of us will admit that he is anything less? From my reading of ancient history, it would seem that when the O'Loughlins and the O'Neills and the O'Briens and the O'Connors were fighting for the crown, when the O'Byrnes were being despoiled and the O'Farrells deposed and the O'Donnells attainted by Parliament, the Gannons and the McIntyres were the only ones who ever had to do a day's work at all. And they are looking for blind obedience! To use a Soviet term, we are deviationists by race.

Then take this pet idea of Marx and Engels that when the proletariat is freed the state will wither away. What Irishman wants to see the state wither away and with it all the grand shenanigans of local and national politics?

But above and beyond all these, the true son of Erin is aroused and repelled by the hard core of atheism, of dialectic materialism, that unifies the theory and practice of the Kremlin. The cruelty of the Soviet and its appeal to certain intellectuals are rooted in its Godlessness. Its success, achieved like Hitler's, mostly through other people's blundering, has been so marked throughout by the mark of the beast, that many regard it as preternatural, something that God allows Hell to accomplish for the chastisement of a faithless modern world. Certain it is that when the beast strikes at last, our hope will lie in those who have been marked with the mark of God's Grace. Whatever can be said of Ireland, good or bad, this must be said: for centuries she has borne in her sacred flesh the mark of the five holy wounds. They were bloody during her long agony of crucifixion, they were shining on the day of her resurrection, and whatever the future may bring of blessings and trials, they will remain to the end the real source of her glory among the nations of the earth.

When Patrick set the new fire of Easter across the valley from Tara, the Wizard rushed to the King and cried, "Unless it is quenched this night when it is lighted, it will not be quenched till Doomsday." And that night it was not quenched. The powers of darkness, looking out toward the West, can see it now through the cracks in the Iron Curtain. From it—who knows?—the ancient light of Russia may one day be rekindled and with it the hope of the world for lasting peace. A toast then to Innisfail, Island of Destiny.

Pride of Race Can Be Overdone

The Friendly Sons of St. Patrick, New York, 1959

May it please Your Eminence, Your Excellencies Most Reverend Bishops, Your Excellency the Governor, Your Honor the Mayor, Deputy Prime Minister of Ireland, Senator Mansfield*—Blessed Mary ever Virgin, Blessed Michael the Archangel, Blessed John the Baptist—and most friendly Sons of St. Patrick:

I have to begin by apologizing for my voice. Unfortunately it's the result of an English fog and not of Irish Mist. For the last five days I have had one foot in the grave. They told me this would be fatal, coming out tonight, but I wanted to die to the strains of "O'Donnell Abu." I wanted to be carried out of the Astor on my shield. Above all, I did not want to miss the 175th Anniversary program. When you celebrated your sesquicentennial—that was twenty-five years ago—I was too young to be out late at night, and when you come to celebrate your bicentennial in 1984 I shall be out of town—permanently. By that time, of course, Pope John XXIII will be just geting his second wind. Cardinal Spellman will be returning from one of his routine trips to the moon where I'm sure he won't be a bit surprised to see Eleanor Roosevelt. She'll be up there, gathering material for her new column, "My Night." But I and a lot of other old gaf-

* Nelson A. Rockefeller, Robert F. Wagner, Sean F. Lemass, Michael J. Mansfield.

fers that are around here will be out of town, and that gives this 175th dinner a special flavor.

This evening as I sat here in excellent company, between the Deputy Prime Minister of Ireland and the Governor of New York, listening to my favorite Glee Club and pretending, like the rest of you loyal hypocrites, to enjoy the Irish bacon and kale, I had been thinking of that first dinner of the Friendly Sons in 1784. They had it in Cape's Tavern downtown—low ceiling, sanded floor, pewter mugs, churchwarden pipes, curtained windows looking out on cobblestones. The brains of the party was Daniel McCormick, who lived on Wall Street and consequently had fifteen terms as president. And helping him was a gallant soldier with the self-effacing name of Hercules Mulligan.

They had gathered together, "a respectable company," to quote the news account, "for an evening of elegant entertainment"—about seventy Irishmen, half of them officers and soldiers in the Continental Army, and most of them left-footers.

The Revolution was over. Peace had been ratified a few months before, the redcoats had sailed home with their tails between their legs. The broken Treaty of Limerick had been avenged at Yorktown, and Washington had entered New York with two Irish generals beside him—Knox and Clinton. But all the fun wasn't over. You see, no constitution had been drafted yet. So Congress had broken up in disgust and nobody knew who was in charge of what. Man dear, the arguments they had! It was a grand time to be alive! There were twenty-eight toasts that night—every one of them, "Bottoms up!" Those Protestants could certainly hold it! The papers said next day that the toasts had all been drunk, but didn't say anything about the Friendly Sons.

Your Silver Anniversary came in 1809, with storm signals raised all along the coast. Austria was fighting Napoleon with English money and the War of 1812 was just around the corner.

But the Golden Jubilee in 1834 was bright and gay, reflecting the age of Andrew Jackson. Industry was on the rise. One thousand miles of railroad had been built; by way of a switch, the railroads were putting the buses out of business, and Mayor Wagner will be surprised, I am sure, to learn the assessed valuation of New York real estate was up to $150 million. That sounds to me like a very small slice of Lincoln Square. On the Diamond Jubilee in 1859 the storm clouds were back again, thicker than ever. John Brown had attacked Harpers Ferry, and the Republicans were about to capture the White House. Dark days, indeed! But the Democratic Party, and Tammany Hall in particular, were already getting a blood transfusion—good green blood, mind you. It was pouring in through Castle Garden. In spite of secession, and impending war, the Friendly Sons felt that the future was bright.

By the time of the Centenary in 1884, everything was serene again. Chester A. Arthur, a self-effacing Republican, had lived down the scandals of the Reconstruction days, and all Grover Cleveland had to do was spend the surplus revenue of his virtuous predecessors. That has a strangely familiar ring at the present time, especially in Albany. The sun was still shining twenty-five years later, in 1909. Good old Teddy Roosevelt was in Africa shooting hippopotamuses—and Taft didn't know yet that he was to be one of them. Of course, nobody dreamed of the First World War.

The Sesquicentennial in 1934 was a depression celebration, but the sun was already breaking through the clouds in Washington. "My friends!" A knight in shining armor, *sans peur et sans reproche,* had just saved the country from the special interests, but while most of us were hailing God's gift to the radio, Al Smith was still unconvinced. He told you that night at the dinner what he thought of brain-trusters and the NRA and alphabet soup in general.

Far off on the horizon three strong men had appeared. Not

good men, not great men—strong men. Men who solved all moral problems in terms of themselves. But nobody in the Astor ballroom gave it a thought. After all, Stalin was busy with another five-year plan; Hitler, the new Chancellor, was busy keeping Stalin out of Germany, and Mussolini was busy keeping Hitler out of Austria. So why worry?

Tonight, however, on your 175th Anniversary, the storm signals are flying again all around us and the sky is dark. Senator Mansfield would say that hurricane signals are flying over Berlin. Fifteen years ago we sowed the wind, and in our headlong flight from the austerities of war we said to England and France, "Let's make believe that the bear that walks like a man is really a man. Let's pretend that he is civilized and capable of good faith. If only this delusion can be maintained long enough, all four of us can occupy Berlin until the world is at peace again." A fool is sometimes punished by life more cruelly than a felon. We sowed the wind and now it looks as if we are about to reap the whirlwind.

But grave as this situation certainly is, it is not the gravest one we face tonight. For even if this hurricane should pass, even if civil war should flare up in the Soviet and the slave states should win their freedom, a greater threat would still remain—the threat that is posed by racism. By "racism" here we do not mean the pride of race, the SANCTA SUPERBIA, that is akin to patriotism, the racism of the Friendly Sons. At all our dinners every speaker is expected to get up in turn and tell the Irish of New York something that they have never heard before—and never even suspected—namely and to wit: that they are the worthy sons of the greatest race on the face of the earth. That's why we come to the dinner. It isn't for the bacon and kale. That's why each member tries to bring with him as his guest a Nordic or a Mediterranean or a Semite. We feel that it is good for their humility.

Of course, nobody knows just what they mean by a "race." Some, for example, classify all human beings by the shape of their skulls. The roundheaded types are Eurasiatic. The long-headed types Eurafrican. There are many of those in the British Isles with long horse-faces and they are very superior indeed. On the dais tonight you will find roundheads and eggheads, and squareheads, and a few flatheads, and every mother's son of them is sure that he belongs to a superior race. Others classify themselvs by their color and by their hair. Look around your table tonight. If the man across from you has straight hair he's a Mongoloid. If it's wooly he is clearly African. If it is curly, he's Indo-European. If it is gone completely, he's out of luck!

And just what race do we think we belong to? We are Celts, of course. And who were the Celts? Let's face it, gentlemen, they were barbarians. In fact, when the ancestors of those Mediterraneans and Semites that you brought with you were eating off silver plate, your ancestors were as wild as Governor Rockefeller's. Of course, they were not simple savages like the Britons, who painted their bodies blue and lived on acorns. They were smart barbarians who could crack heads as well as jokes, and who, starting from the foot of the Alps, conquered everybody in sight from the Atlantic to the Black Sea.

About the time when Rome was getting a start and Greece was already past her prime, the Celts attacked Ireland and took it away from the natives. They went in, as the Normans did later in England, as overlords, or kings, or to use the term we are more familiar with, as mayors. They made up the budgets and took up the taxes and saw to it that nobody was satisfied. Only a few of them stayed in the country after the fighting was over. But the curious fact is that, from then on, the kings were the only ones that had any children. The simple taxpayers, who weren't very bright, and were known then as now as the aborigines, have almost no descendants alive today. Where they exist, simple folk like the Gannons and the Farleys and the Hanrahans, they are known as the thick Irish. But there are so few of us left in America today that we are collectors' items, and it does us no end of good to spend this blessed evening with Cardinal Spellman and the rest of you pure Celts. God love you! That last remark is copyrighted.

Race, therefore, is not nearly as tangible a thing as nationality. I am not quite sure what a race is, but I know that a nation is a moral union of families working together for the good of all. And when I realize that I am indebted to you, my neighbors, for public safety and public decency, that it is you, my neighbors, who make it possible for me to sleep in my bed at night and go to my church on Sunday, I am conscious of a bond of mutual gratitude that transcends the accident of color, hair, and shape of another's skull.

The sad fact that the white man lost that consciousness for so many centuries, while building up his colonial empires, has brought about the present threat, which is more serious in the long run than communism. For racism in its worst form, that is, not pride of race, but hatred of another race, is sweeping through the world like a prairie fire. The blacks and yellows and browns are on the march, and nobody knows where they are going. They don't know themselves. They only know that by sheer force of numbers, countless millions of them—four-fifths of the human race—they can eventually force their former masters into the sea.

So that even if the Asiatics in Moscow and Peiping became capitalists tomorrow and communism vanished from the earth, the ultimate threat of racism would remain.

How, then, do we face the storm as Sons of the Gael? We face it with a double advantage. Our own bitter past and the degrading injustice of centuries gives us a feeling for the underdog everywhere in the world. Can't we put that to work before the deluge comes, and persuade all races, at least in the United States, to submerge their sense of race in a glorious sense of nationhood? It will be only when non-whites feel as much at home in America as we do, that we can offer any leadership to the rest of the world. Our country should be a model of racial harmony instead of a by-word, for we have no common origin that would make others feel like outsiders here. We have no history of a single tradition of religion as they have in Europe, but only the tremendous bond of living and working together for the good of all. That should be enough. Let's hope it is.

But in any case we shall hold on to our Irish optimism and remember the ups and downs of the 175 years just passed, the sunshine, the clouds, the sunshine again. By the law of averages the bicentennial in 1984 should be free from the shadow of disaster. That sounds just like the Irish, doesn't it? Yes, and thank God it does. Since the days of St. Patrick we have been brought up on hope (sometimes it was all our fathers had to live on), supernatural hope, by which we always knew that no matter what happened our story would eventually end with the words, "And he lived happily ever after." We may have a strain of melancholy deep in our hearts, but never a suspicion of despair. That is because our Irish optimism rests on divine justice, not delusions. We'll always be able to tell any poor man we meet that he can live happily ever after, because he can.

So, St. Patrick, keep us in your holy prayers and don't forget the Nordics and the Mediterraneans and the Semites. It is no fault of theirs that they're not Irish!

More Blarney, Please

The Friendly Sons of St. Patrick, San Diego, 1961

AS THE old bard in Tara used to say, "There are three mortal things that cannot be improved upon: the flight of a sea gull over the water, a winter sky full of stars, and the soft tongue of an Irish toastmaster." When the Irish toastmaster has lived for years on the Mexican border, where he could watch the toreadors plying their trade, he has a natural bent for one of the most important skills that Ireland has given the world—blarney. For it is Irish, it is a skill, and it is important, never more so than now.

If you thumb your *Oxford Dictionary*—and let us not be narrow-minded about this thing—you will find that while "lie" and "fraud" and "cheat" and "flatter" are all Middle English in origin, "blarney," which does not mean the same as any one of them, is the Gaelic for groves. Its deep significance, however, comes from the first Lord of the Groves—the first Lord of Blarney. That was Cormac McDonald Carty. Four hundred years ago, Carty was over in London to work out a little deal with Queen Elizabeth. One of her henchmen was trying to get him to change the traditional system by which the clans elected their chief and to install voting machines. But Carty felt as Frank Hague of Jersey City always felt about the unreliability of a machine, so to cut the argument short, he said with a twinkle in his eye and the devil about the corners of his mouth, "Go tell that virgin Queen of yours—" He got no further. The English roared, "Now we know there is no truth in the man. 'Tis all blarney it is." And blarney it was!

In the years that have passed since then, blarney has developed from a flash of genius to a fine art. A coarse and unfeeling Saxon might call it a lie (and to be honest 'tis not the whole truth and nothing but the truth!). But 'tis not a lie. 'Tis not even one of those mysterious mental reservations that the Dominicans are famous for. Perhaps then it is a white lie? His Excellency the Bishop, as a good moral theologian, will tell you there is no such thing. *What about a green lie?* Oh, a green lie! Now we are discussing poetry, for real blarney is a poetic rearrangement of facts mutually understood. It would be something like diplomacy if diplomats had any conscience and a sense of humor. For example: I go to a cottage door and knock. An old granny of eighty-five puts her nose through the crack, and I say, "Good morning, dear. Is your mother about?" Blarney!

Of course, if we asked one of your sensitive lawyers for a definition of the term, his delicate nose might detect some slight odor of fraud in all this. "Fraud," he would say, with great precision, "is a representation of fact, consciously untrue, made with the purpose of causing another to act and resulting in damage. There are company frauds, banking frauds, mail frauds, shell games, the handkerchief game, amateur athletics, income tax returns and television repairs. Now blarney (he would say) differs from all of these only in this, that it does not result in damage." So much for the limitations of the highest legal talent. You know as well as I do that there are many fine distinctions besides, that might not appear in the thick fog that surrounds a modern trial, but suppose for the sake of argument that there is here a harmless affinity with fraud. That only makes the blarney more important. For then it becomes an antitoxin to be injected into the veins of a modern society which is sick unto death with the toxin.

Our age has been called many things besides the Atomic Age, and none is a better fit than the Age of Fraud. Was there ever a time when we had such a predominant majority of fakers in public and private life? Was there ever a time when more nations were playing a shell game, when high-sounding slogans meant less?

Forty-odd years ago, our Age of Innocence in the United States, the age of Richard Harding Davis and Lillian Russell, came to a close with an ex-college president in the White House. I have no particular prejudice against college presidents—still less against ex-college presidents—some of them are as smart as a pastor, but they all have a weakness for swinging a slogan by the tail, and slogans are a breeding ground for fraud. So it was with Woodrow Wilson. He proclaimed that we were to enter the World War he had been elected for keeping us out of, not to preserve the British Empire—Heaven forbid! (Walter Hines Page, our Ambassador at the Court of St. James's, was the only one who was in on that.) No. We went to war to make the world safe for democracy by the great principle of the self-determination of nations! We all tossed our hats in the air and shouted "Hurrah for us!" But unfortunately the whole thing turned out to be a fraud. Self-determination was to be a weapon of vengeance used to destroy those who were not on the inside. Versailles was another fraud. It was not a peace conference at all. It was a Roman holiday for secret societies, so that when the Big Four got through with self-determination, it was such a success, and made the world so safe for democracy that the war begun in 1914 is still going on.

By 1941 the Great White Father was reigning in the White House—at such times as Eleanor was on the road! What a college president he would have made! What commencement speeches! What slogans! What budgets! Years before when he was serving under Wilson on a dry ship in the Navy, he had seen the German Empire cleverly undermine the Russian Empire, not with guns but with a gigantic fraud called Communism —a philosophy of government that flourishes by selling stock in a nonexistent gold mine. Twenty years later, Germany, fearing the fraud that had already engulfed Russia, developed an antibody, a counterfraud called Nazism. When this fraud and counterfraud had resolved themselves into a bloody vortex, we got in the fight to make certain that the victorious fraud would be the weaker one. Thereby we assured the survival of the fraud that has dominated all our thinking ever since.

Having won the war, we proceeded to lose the peace through another fraud perpetrated under the spell of previous frauds. This one was staged in San Francisco and was a huge social success. Two thousand, seven hundred and eighty-four people came together from fifty different countries. Their eloquence covered seventy-eight tons of paper in spite of the fact that Ireland was excluded. The press and radio sent 2,636 publicity experts to report every golden word, of which there were sometimes 1,700,000 a day. Even here in California where you do things in a big way, it was considered a generous discussion and adequate coverage. But up on Nob Hill, a small group in a smoke-filled room drew up the Charter of the United Nations and carefully planted in its heart a cynical fraud called the Yalta Formula. This was the famous veto plan that disfranchised for ten years five of the most civilized countries on the face of the earth while reducing most of the rest to an expensive debating society. Now they don't even debate. They pound their desks with their shoes. The President of the United States, good old Harry, started them off with his usual *joie de vivre*. It was more fun for Harry than the Potsdam Conference, but most responsible Americans have done a lot of worrying ever since.

So today, surrounded by international fraud, we live in a world of fear. It has had an effect on our personal peace, our industrial peace, our domestic peace, and even our religious peace. We have a series of undeclared wars around us at every level. Superficial students of the Irish character might think that a state of war is not entirely repugnant to us. But they don't know how to distinguish. Broken heads are all right, if they are carefully selected in certain parts of Belfast and not broken beyond repair, but broken treaties, broken homes and broken hearts are different altogether, and it is mostly because of these that we suggest a little blarney to take the poison out of an Age of Fraud. Blarney, of course, is not the final solution of anything. It is merely the lubricant that keeps the machinery running until we can find a solution. In the present international crisis it can probably do very little. The Chinese are better at it than we are, and the Russians can't understand it at all. The Israelis have been selling suits trimmed with blarney for two thousand years. The difficulty is that the Arabs don't seem to be buying them. But on the home front, blarney could help so much in our labor wars if management and the boys in the shops would cover their sharp teeth once in a while with a smile. It would help keep families together. If John would only tell Mary often enough how young and pretty she is, and Mary would tell John that he is clever and masterful, they would both be happier for laughing up their sleeves. And the same thing is true at the church level. A little blarney among them and the Catholics, Protestants and Jews would be surprised to find out how much charity there is just around the corner. No one would say that Good Pope John knew anything about blarney—but the Archbishop of Canterbury certainly went home walking on air.

If, however, you are still inclined to be scrupulous about a green lie that is no lie at all, and apprehensive about the eternal consequences, just remember what the Irish can expect at the Last Judgment. The great Saint Patrick used to spend the Holy Season of Lent, not in a luxury hotel like this, eating shrimp and filet mignon washed down with everything except Bushmills, but up on the very top of Croagh Patrick in County Mayo. His fast was no easy modern mortification, full of calories and vitamins, but a good old black Irish fast that knocked a man out for the rest of the year. When Lent was over, an angel appeared—it was the least he could do—and by way of reward, assured him that his prayer was heard and that the Irish would never lose the Faith. "Thanks be to God," said the Saint, "but there's another little matter I'd like you to handle for me. On the Last Day I'd like to sit in judgment over the Chosen People." Don't laugh! He didn't mean what you mean. He meant his own. He had read in the Gospels how the twelve Apostles would judge the twelve tribes of Israel, and felt that the Irish deserved the same kind of a break; an admirable principle still observed in New York in the naming of all our judges. When you come before Patrick then, if blarney is the worst thing on your record, you can look for a halo sparkling with emeralds.

Tonight then is no time for pessimism. It is no time to regard universal peace and universal integrity as an illusion. Rather, we apply the Theory of Limits that we learned in our classes of arithmetic. We are never going to arrive at perfection, but we can always get twice as close. Meanwhile, we are ready for the worst and hope for the best. Who knows? The world crisis will pass in ten or fifteen years. The clouds of fraud will melt away like the mist in the Gap of Dunloe. The integrity of the American people will shine through their government. Our own way of life will become a beacon light for the human race. Homes and workshops and churches will glow with charity, ushering in a golden age when frauds will be the exception.

Of course it's all blarney—but isn't it grand?

We Knew the Happy Warrior

The Friendly Sons of St. Patrick, New York, 1963

I AM GRATEFUL to President Hughes and a very kind fate that at long last I can respond to the toast, "*The United States.*" For the first time in my life the other speaker of the evening has assumed the grave responsibility of presenting Ireland in a way that will satisfy everybody present: the real Irish, the sentimental third generation, the wistful half Irish (Mayor Wagner, will you take a bow?), as well as the Mediterraneans, the Medes and the Persians that always flatter us by getting in on the party. This, Ambassador Boland* has accomplished with a skill worthy of his diplomatic training in the land of the soft tongue. He has shown us that Kathleen Ni Houlahan can be a shrewd calculating member of the United Nations though she still has, on a special occasion like this, a smile and a tear in her eye, while dear little Molly Malone has become a European Power interested in the Common Market.

For twenty-five years now, since 1937, it has been my privilege to celebrate so often this celebrated "Day We Celebrate" that I had completely run out of celebrities. I had seen that Minstrel Boy off to the war much too often and yet it looked as if I would never get a chance at the second toast. But this year when they went to the White House as usual to ask them to nominate a substitute for the President, Caroline suggested me. She is one

* Frederick H. Boland, Irish representative to the U.N.

figure in public life that I can understand. She adds and subtracts the same way that I do, and she always says exactly what she thinks. For example, she thinks that Washington, D.C., is the most interesting zoo in the world—and so do I.

I was just about her age when I went to live there myself for six eventful years. At that time it was a city of red brick houses and horse cars. Curious little stage coaches called herdicks still drove up and down Sixteenth Street past our house. Don't jump to conclusions! It was after the Civil War. The family had left New York in 1897 because my father—who was not entirely French—had lost a fight. In spite of everything he could do to stop it, the B.&O. Railroad had capitulated to the Standard Oil and had sold the Staten Island Ferry to a certain Colonel Rogers who was a partner of the Governor's extravagant grandfather. This famous bearded colonel had promptly turned them over for a consideration to City Hall—or should I say to a Chinaman named Richard Croker, the leader of a Japanese organization whose name escapes me at the moment. There was a certain amount of pressure and profit all around, though of course the municipality has been losing money ever since. As a direct result of the deal, an indignant young idealist of forty-five transferred from the B.&O. to the Southern Railroad, with headquarters on Pennsylvania Avenue.

When we arrived from New York that spring, the shouting was over and so was the inauguration, but there were still slogans plastered everywhere, urging us to elect William Jennings Bryan to the presidency so that we could all have free silver. I did not know what that meant—nobody seemed to know—and it would be years before I would appreciate the theme song always so popular in Washington, "The Best Things in Life Are Free."

So Cleveland was out and McKinley was in, but everything was safe because there was still a touch of green at the President's desk. Cleveland's mother had been Baltimore Irish, so it was too bad to lose him, but McKinley's grandfather, Jim, had come over from Conagher in County Antrim. Unfortunately his successor, Theodore Roosevelt, was destined to be the last Republican to bring a dash of aristocracy to the White House. It was only a dash. The poor man wasn't even half Irish—I think he was an octoroon—but he had enough good blood in him to be an honorary member of this Society. That doesn't mean that we should hold anything against Harding and Coolidge and Eisenhower because their poor ancestors were just a lot of honest foreigners. They were decent people too. We must be reasonable about this thing. The whole human race can't be descended from kings. But we have to admit that no matter what else can be said, most modern Democrats have had one conspicuous distinction. Wilson had a grandfather, Jim, who came over from Strabane in Tyrone (though of course that was never stressed in the Princeton yearbook) and even F.D.R. himself was Irish by marriage. I don't mean that Eleanor was exactly what you would call a colleen bawn, but she did marry the man on the Seventeenth of March. And now, of course, we have the royal strain undiluted.

With McKinley's election, then, my interest in public affairs began, and I formed the early habit of eating my dessert every night, standing fascinated beside my father's chair, absorbing youthful impressions about the United States: the impression for example that Bryan was a madman; that Democrats in general were irresponsible and would ruin the country if they won another national election—which didn't seem likely; that on the other hand, the Republican Mark Hanna was a brazen rascal, every bit as bad as Samuel Gompers; that the War Department was thoroughly corrupt, and that McKinley himself was a spineless figurehead who was shot just in time to save his reputation. As you probably suspect by now, my father was a Friendly Son of St. Patrick, so that his views were always inclined to be neutral and colorless. On the credit side he was convinced that Teddy Roosevelt and Cardinal Gibbons were God's gift to the nation and that the Irish could still save America and mold it to their own image and likeness if only they would remain true to themselves. It broke his heart to see some of them making municipal government a byword of corruption and some of them surrendering to snobbery, changing their names and trying to forget their cultural heritage.

For culturally it was a critical time for us in 1897. The really hard days were over. The persecution and ridicule of the Irish had died down, though the American Protective Association was a very recent memory and people in the streets were still singing, "Here lies the Mick who threw the brick. He'll never throw another. For calling me an A.P.A., he now lies under cover." (I shouldn't have tried to sing that! There goes my last chance to make the Glee Club!) But the Molly Maguires and the Orange riots and the squalor of Five Points were definitely past. In spite of the progress, however, the United States as a whole had no idea as yet how much it owed to the Irish race and people still talked glibly about "the good old days of thrift and integrity before the Irish came." Evidently the country still needed distinguished historians of the nineteenth century who would ask, "What good old days? Name two!" The politics of those good old days they bragged about make ours look angelic and the memoirs of sniffing English visitors like Charles Dickens give us some idea of our culture in the 1820's and 30's. Of course, when we say that the new nation needed the Irish we must not exaggerate. After all, we don't have to canonize a whole race even on the Seventeenth of March. Plenty of individuals have disgraced us over the years, but the point we make is that, by and large, the Irish have always at least *leaned* to the side of the angels and their descendants in the United States have continued to *lean* in the same direction.

There are living examples all around me at this glittering head table who could be singled out for applause, but no one with a drop of royal blood would want to hear himself praised in public! So one who is here tonight only in *spirit* must serve as a symbol of what the United States owes to the Irish immigrant.

Imagine, then, that here on the dais where he sat out dinner after dinner, waiting to make the last speech and wave to Katie who was always listening in from the top balcony—imagine that you see the Happy Warrior himself; not the bitter, disillusioned Al of the middle thirties but the mellow philosopher of the forties or, better still, the dashing, magnetic, lovable leader who was given fifteen million enthusiastic votes for the highest office in the land.

I happened to be in England in 1928 but was able to follow the campaign with breathless interest because all England was following it the same way. *The Times* of London ("Are there any other *Times?*") which printed only four pages of news including the court calendar, broke all precedent by reporting day by day the speeches of this man Smith. Every time I entered the Combination Room of a College in Cambridge someone would say, "What chance has this extraordinary chap?" And I would answer, "He's the next President of the United States. First, because he is all man in a world full of boloney, and second, because he embodies for everyone with a handicap, the great and consoling truth that in the United States all handicaps are surmountable for anyone with a head and a heart." Then I would go on to describe how Al's whole life was a steeplechase, one obstacle after another, each one apparently increasing his zest for the race. I pictured for them a fatherless little boy brought up in the shadow of Brooklyn Bridge with very little schooling and a name so common that he was practically anonymous, just another Smith; the Fulton Fish Market; the temptations of the old Fourth Ward; machine politics in the days of their glory—and what price glory! What could anyone expect from such a background but another Big Boss

Tweed? And yet we got the Happy Warrior. Why? Because his mother had raised him with the deep Faith of the Irish and a profound love for the American way of life. The slums, instead of corrupting him, gave his personality warmth and color; the fish market, instead of deadening his ambitions, gave him a spirit of study. He was never a cultured man. His grammar was a little uncertain to the end. But in 1915 Elihu Root could say that he knew more about the State of New York than any man alive, and ten years later the same could almost be said with regard to the United States. He was never a plaster saint. He was a politician all his life; never got to Washington where he might have been mistaken for a statesman. From his early days in the assembly he knew all about horse trading, could throw his weight around in a caucus and smoke cigars with the kind of people all practical politicians smoke cigars with. It was even rumored that he was once seen taking a drink. But except for the stories that bubbled up out of the pit in 1928, his worst enemies never questioned his integrity or his patriotism. As for the handicap of his name, although there are 230 Smiths in *Who's Who,* 4,000 in the Manhattan Directory, and the *Encyclopaedia Britannica* devotes twelve pages to the clan, "Smith" today in the U.S.A. means nobody else but Al! That sounds like a good commercial on the "raddio"!

When the end came in 1944, he was probably sharing in the irrational optimism that was already abroad. The tide of the war had turned and we were confident of ultimate victory. We knew that we were fighting the only bad men in existence. We knew that our democratic allies in Moscow were going to be a big help in setting up the brave new world and the only thing we had to fear was fear itself.

It might come as a shock to Al if he were back with us now in his ninetieth year, to find the United States plunged into an equally irrational pessimism. Wars and rumors of wars are all about us. Collective bargaining approaching a crisis with a public that is losing its patience. Our highest courts engaged in the strangest speculations; our schools producing problems instead of solving them; our juvenile crime showing a percentage increase that is terrifying at a time when juvenile crime is decreasing in Dublin.

But in the midst of all this gloom, can't you hear Al's familiar grunt? "Let's look at the record." For instance, what about our form of government? The equality of men as persons still leaves something to be desired, but integration has certainly advanced in twenty years and the supremacy of the law over the ruler is still intact. Democracy, then, is far from dead. Our standards of living are higher than ever before, and we do not refer to TV and frozen food. We mean that the United States is still in the eyes of all the world a land of opportunity. Higher education with all its faults is more available to the talented poor boy now than ever before. Our courts are still dispensing basic justice and even if some of our judges are a little hazy about the natural law, corruption is exceptional, while the nearest thing we have to a secret police is the glorious F.B.I., of which we are so justly proud.

After all this the victim of 1928 would remark with one of his biggest grins showing every tooth in his head, that religious bitterness is rapidly becoming a thing of the past. What with Good Pope John in the Vatican and Caroline in the White House, the more advanced of our separated brethren will take a chance now even on a Jesuit.

So if this great American who owed so much to his Irish antecedents, were standing at this lectern tonight he would say with deep faith in the God of his fathers and love for the land of his birth, "The record of the United States is still a record worth looking at."

V

AFTERMATHS OF WAR

The Dutch Love Peace

The Netherlands-America Foundation and the Chamber of Commerce of the State of New York, New York, 1947

FORTY years ago, when Dr. van Kleffens* was a youngster of thirteen playing around the lakes of Friesland, a fourteen-year-old American boy was paying his first and last visit to The Hague. He drove out by horse and carriage to the House in the Woods where the young Queen usually spent her summers, and stood in the driveway listening with awe while his elders told him what was going on behind closed doors. The Second Peace Conference was in progress—forty-four states were represented—some of them for the first time from Latin America, and as a result of their deliberations there would never be another great war. It made a deep impression on me, for I was the boy, of course—and from that day to this I have thought of the Netherlands every time I have thought of universal and lasting peace.

It is true that the inspiration for The Hague Conference came from Russia, the benighted Russia of the Tsars. It opened its first session on the Tsar's birthday, with the Russian Ambassador presiding, and we have it on good authority that he was heard distinctly several times saying "yes." It was only later that the word vanished from the language. The principal point in the Russian program was the voluntary reduction of armament, and unfortunately, though many other things were

* Eelco N. van Kleffens, former Minister of Foreign Affairs of the Netherlands and Netherlands representative on the U.N. Security Council.

accomplished by the Conference, there was little progress with the principal point. For those were the dark ages, when power politics determined international relations. Forty years ago rulers were more concerned with the balance of power than with the laws of God, and as there was some suspicion in the world before democracy was universal, no one dared to lay down the first howitzer. The Second Conference ended with the intention of meeting again in eight years—but eight years later was 1915 and the League of Nations was just around a very bloody corner.

Notwithstanding all of that, however, I still feel justified in linking universal peace with The Hague rather than with Geneva or even the Flushing Meadows. For 1907 saw the last family gathering of the nations with everyone there who wanted to be there. It was the last Thanksgiving dinner with everybody welcome and everything free. By the time the palace in Geneva was built, the nations had been divided into the damned and the canonized—neatly, but always with complete partiality. A suspicion lingered in the minds of certain skeptics that sanctity had something to do with military success. Still, who knows, it might have worked except for the fact that the holiest and most successful of the canonized preferred to remain in the outer darkness with the damned. But even today, when we have joined the saints and can pray with Outer Mongolia for the conversion of backward nations like Ireland, now when we can watch the Capital of the World rise into the clouds from Forty-second Street with all the pride of New Yorkers born of New Yorkers, we still miss The Hague and the quiet dignity of "The House in the Woods" where everybody was welcome and everything was free.

Of course, the impression made on a fourteen-year-old boy may have influenced a tired old man—but not as much, I am sure, as the things he has learned about the Dutch in the intervening years. To begin with, he has found that they have a traditional interest in world peace running back for centuries. There was Erasmus of Rotterdam, with his "Complaint of Peace" and his dream of a congress of Kings to be held at Cambrai; and the great Hugo Grotius of Delft, who earned the title of "The Father of International Law" for his book *De Jure Belli et Pacis,* with its noble appeal for a Congress of Christian Powers. But we need not go further back than thirty years, when the Dutch Anti-War Council went to work on the Central Organization for a Durable Peace. Their country was formed by the deltas of two great rivers, the Maas and the Rhine, on whose crest throughout the Middle Ages flowed most of the commerce of Central Europe and the East to England. In the golden seventeenth century, the Netherlands was the greatest commercial center of the world and the Dutch the shrewdest business men. It is true that about this time they exchanged New York for Surinam in South America, but they couldn't know that Tammany Hall was going to put the city on its feet—and besides, it was done at the point of an English blunderbus. Left to themselves, they did pretty well—and the campus of Fordham University stands today as a monument to one of them, a certain John Acer, who bought the Fordham Manor, about 1660. This was, at the time, a tidy piece of some 10,000 acres, comprising the best part of Jimmy Lyons Borough of Universities, and he got the Mohicans to part with for an anker of rum and six coats of duffles.

A more important quality, however, than a mere knack for trading has been their honest thrift. No people in history, perhaps, have done more to build their own country than the Dutch. We Americans found a continent stretching from ocean to ocean—3,000 miles of incredible wealth, and starting from the Atlantic wasted our resources prodigally. They found two deltas of marshland and made them a garden—a nation—an empire. Inch by inch they redeemed the land from the water, impoldering it with their windmills for centuries. The whole world applauded the project of the Zuider Zee and cried out with indignation when the dikes were wrecked and salt water ruined hundreds of square miles of polder—of fertile land. But the Dutch not only know how to save. What is a more important element of thrift, they know how to spend. In the Netherlands budget of 1940, the only item higher than national defense was the sum allotted to education, art and science.

Up to this point, we have referred only to the self-regarding virtues of shrewdness and thrift. Valuable as they are, they would not suffice to make the Netherlands a natural leader in the quest of world peace. But added to these qualities we find a national attitude toward the rest of the human race which appears in the individual Dutchman as Christian charity. Let this be a shining example of what I mean. Way back in the seventeenth century, when all Europe was an armed camp of battling sects, when Protestants feared and hated above all things this side of Hell a Catholic religious order called the Jesuits, when hysterical Englishmen were racking, hanging, drawing and quartering every man like me they could lay their hands on—here in the New World French Jesuits and Dutch traders were peacefully rubbing elbows up along the Mohawk Trail. Father Isaac Jogues, who had been mutilated and enslaved by the savages, was dragged over from Ossernenon to Fort Orange on a trading expedition. There he was befriended by a Dutch Reformed Minister—Dominie Joannes Megapolensis, who sent him food from his own table and clothed him and persuaded the captain of the fort to rescue him. The captain placated the Indians with gifts, worth 300 livres, and the Protestant sailors on a Dutch ship in the Hudson risked their lives in carrying a Jesuit priest to New Amsterdam on the Island of Manahatte. Here Governor Kieft received him kindly—lodged him and fed him for three months until he could arrange his passage back to Europe. What would have been his fate in the Colony of Massachusetts, where even the simple Quakers were lashed at the tail of a cart? The story of how this Protestant minister and all the

Dutch Protestants of the Colony befriended not only Isaac Jogues but other Jesuit missionaries who crossed their trail—seeing Christ in people who worshiped in a different church—forms one of the most beautiful chapters in our colonial history.

But even in their love for humanity we have not reached the principal reason for linking the Dutch with universal peace. Of supreme importance is their well-earned reputation for placing principle above expediency. Many examples could be cited over the centuries, but to keep within the memory of Dr. van Kleffens go back to the time of his graduation from the University of Leyden. Holland was desperately poor. Her seaborne trading had been wiped out and the people were down to the barest necessities of life. The Dutch were just as unpopular with the Allies in the first part of the World War as the Irish were in the second part, and for the same reason—they had declined to commit suicide. But now their chance had come to jump on the bandwagon and share in the spoils of peace. The Yankees were arriving in overwhelming numbers; the tide had definitely turned; the defeat of the Central Powers might come any time. But there was no last-minute hypocrisy. The Dutch let the bandwagon pass them by and merely tightened their belts. Worse than that, they outraged the sensibilities of the victors by giving sanctuary to the vanquished and humiliated Kaiser at Doorn.

That was not, of course, a mark of German sympathy. They had known all along that a German victory would have made them economic slaves. It was rather their unwavering devotion to an ancient ideal already growing dim and now extinguished—international law.

So after V-J Day, when, as after every great war, peace plans began to multiply, some thought that the world would turn to a people known through history as thrifty traders who loved humanity and principle. Some thought that the Netherlands might take a leading role in the decisions to be made by the United Nations. But unfortunately, that distinguished group, when formed, proved to be a realistic organization where no small nation could take a leading role. The vaunted democratic spirit for which we had fought a bitter war was ruled out once and for all in international affairs. But at least we can say that of the little, disfranchized nations who had so much unselfish wisdom to contribute, the brilliant Dutch Foreign Minister was the ablest spokesman. He could not prevent the surrender at San Francisco, but he could and did speak to the people of the world over the heads of their representatives, protesting "dictation by the powerful, the influential and the few," pointing out that the iniquitous veto "flouts the democratic principle" and "consecrates the fallacy that the greatest wisdom is to be found with the greatest number of guns."

He knew full well that this fallacy was not a new one. It was the moral weakness of the old balance of power. The Concert of Europe disregarded small nations in its effort to preserve the peace among great powers. So now, the veto, though introduced by naïve Americans, was so eagerly endorsed by the Soviet that it became suspect. It became a symbol of mere expediency which is the rejection of all principle and as such has at last begun to trouble the remnants of our modern consciences. What we learned the hard and stupid way Dr. van Kleffens knew from the beginning and pointed out with fearlessness and eloquence.

For this and many other things we thank our guest of honor at his parting. He has admirably typified an admirable people and returns to The Hague with our warm admiration. There we feel sure he will continue to fight the unending battle of principle-versus-expediency, on the outcome of which are centered all our prayers and all our hopes for civilization.

The Want of the World

New York Herald Tribune Forum, New York, 1949

IT IS often remarked that a man in Switzerland can understand a man in Java more readily than he can a woman in his own household, and something similar can be said for men themselves in different age groups. As American boys and girls, it is easy for you to understand the general sense of values that prevails at your age in any part of the world together with the hatreds and loyalties that are based on it. Only an exceptional man, however, can remember why some things seemed so vital to him thirty years ago. That is the reason why fathers and sons are so often apart; why one generation underestimates another. The underestimation, of course, is usually mutual. To the youngsters the elders are hopelessly stupid, and to the elders, the youngsters are crazy (and much can be said for both points of view). But old and young should remember that the passage of years has two inevitable effects on mortal man. It dulls his perception and deepens his understanding. So that in planning for the future, you fresh recruits can help us by showing us your visions—visions that for some of us have faded into the light of common day—and we can help you by telling you how veterans interpret them.

Now, in every discussion preliminary to the blueprint of your brave new world, there is always the assumption that your fathers were to blame for getting us involved in World War II, and your grandfathers in World War I. In making this assumption you are playing favorites. You are sparing the real culprits, your grandfathers' grandfathers and maybe their grandfathers before them. For all this horror which we old orange pulps have lived through twice and which is entirely too familiar to these visiting students from far-off places, did not result even principally from the willfulness of tyrants or the stupidity of messianic democrats. Our plight is much more the result of the philosophy that made it possible for our supermen to arrive at their fatal decisions. So it is not going to do you or the world any good to talk about freedom from this, that, or the other things, as long as we are enslaved by this stultifying philosophy.

It is called Naturalism—an innocent name for an appalling affliction. Through it we have inherited the intellectual arrogance of the nineteenth century and with it a spirit of despair. William James was right when he wrote, "Sadness lies at the heart of every natural philosophy." For Naturalism teaches that there is nothing supernatural, nothing spiritual, nothing to hope for. It has a kind of catechism all its own, for it is, in the last analysis, a kind of perverted religion. Its first question reads, "Who made man?" and the answer, "Nobody. He just happened." To the second question, "What then is his purpose in life?" There are two answers, one for each side of the Iron Curtain, but both of them leading to the same sad conclusion. On one side, the Eastern side, the answer reads, "Man lives to promote the interest of the State." On the other side, our side, "Man lives to promote his own health, culture and comfort."

To us, it is clear enough without proof, and clearer still to the poor wretches who live in the Soviet and its dependencies, that life lived for the State is not worth living. Now it is beginning to dawn on us here, in the free part of the world, that the same is true of a life that is lived for our own health, culture and comfort. For if that is all we have to aim at, few can hope for even a shadow of happiness. For most of the human race, health is precarious, culture is on the wane and comfort has vanished. Even the favored few cannot enjoy all three for long.

Besides, how can we expect the happiness of fulfillment when we are living for something that is dead—something that has been dead from its beginning; something that was stillborn? I mean the world. Not the world of the good green earth; the world of the fjords, of the Côte d'Or, of the Delectable Duchy and Rocky Mountains. Not the world of human souls which is the world you are planning for today. I mean the world that Christ refused to pray for; the world which symbolizes self; the world we speak of when we say, the spirit of the world—the World, the Flesh and the Devil. I mean human society insofar as it ignores God's claims, treats God's creatures as its playthings and makes health, culture and comfort the rule of life. That world is dead. As Martha said of her brother Lazarus when he had been in the tomb four days, "*Jam foetet.*" By this time, it stinketh. You can call in the smartest of moderns to strew the house with literary lilies and gardenias but you cannot hide the odor of inner death. The stench of a dead soul has gone all through society; a stench more pungent than the stench of last week's battlefield. It began by poisoning the air which a spiritual people must breathe to live. It ended by conditioning the people through despair for the Absolute State.

So as you sit here today in the ballroom of this great hotel planning for the world you want, be sure you begin with the want of the world, the world of human souls. What that world wants most of all is hope and the will to live; not merely to exist, but to live a full and healthy intellectual and spiritual life, a life that will help it to come finally to grips with the spirit of Naturalism, the spirit of despair.

It is easy of course to exaggerate in a time of crisis. After all, we are not the first generation to have smelt decadence in the air. If we think we are, it is reassuring to read the Old Testament occasionally and sermons that run back to the time of Saint Augustine. In them shall we find that prophets and preachers have always liked to begin with the words, "There never was a time when. . . ." before describing a condition that existed a dozen times before they were born. Fortunately, or rather providentially, there is always an element in society too young for discouragement. Some of my generation knew Europe before the First World War—I paid my first visit forty-five years ago. The conditions we found were not perfect, of course. They never are. There were social injustices, discrimination and poverty—more in some countries than in others. But to the casual observer, that is to the average man, there was culture and beauty and charm, and above all there was order, an order largely entrusted to the keeping of an empire which hardly realized that Victoria was dead. There was a tranquillity of order known as peace which had not been disturbed, except locally, since the Congress of Vienna. Here in America the prospect was so comfortable and so dull that we who were in college at the time used to lament our fate that we had lived too late to see history in the making. With such a background, it requires a conscious effort on our part to realize that something can be salvaged from the wreck of civilization. Your generation has a different point of view. You were born into chaos. It is part of the Providence of God that you, our sons and daughters, who have to pick up the pieces of the Modern Age, should look on disorder and uncertainty as a normal condition to be faced without surprise or fear.

Your elders, perhaps, have seen more disaster than you have, but if you can free yourselves from the philosophy that paralyzed their resistance, if you can realize your own absolute value and your relative value, that is, if you can understand the reason for your dignity as persons, if you can see clearly how you fit into the pattern of creation and why you are here, you will know more about disaster than your grandfathers did, for you will be able to see through disaster. You will be able to hope. For you there will be no delusion that "All's right with the world," but merely the conviction that "God's in His Heaven," which is a very different thing. You will expect the times to be frequently out of joint. You will expect as much regress as progress in the affairs of men. You will be prepared to find that there are some clouds that have no silver lining except what come to them from the white light of eternity; that there are some roads that have no turning this side of the grave. You will not have the heart to tell every poor man you meet that his ship will surely come in some day, because it probably will not. Most ships never do. And yet you will keep your souls alive and keep society alive with hope. And you will look life squarely in the eye and say, "Life is bitter." Of course it is, stupid. What did you expect? Life is a warfare. But who ever said that this little round of weeks and months and years, with its monotony, its disillusionments and its heartbreaks—whoever said this was the whole story? "Only the fool who hath said in his heart there is no God."

When you go to the University, you may run into a Spengler, and historians can be very gloomy indeed, but you will find that history itself is full of hope, full of dawning and of turning tides; full of recurring springtime and of youth. You are the dawn of the world and the turning of the tide. We need you, not for what you know but for what you are. You can supply the want of the world. It is the only way you will ever get the world you want.

Paths to Peace

Convention of Middle States Association,
Atlantic City, 1952

IN SUGGESTING "Paths to Peace" as our subject this evening, your chairman probably hoped to sidetrack a curriculum battle or a clash on methods that might have been appropriate for the eightieth birthday of William Heard Kilpatrick. There was a time when no convention was complete without a tilt between the University of Chicago and Morningside Heights; between traditionalism and progressivism; between Thomas Aquinas, alias Robert Hutchins, alias Mortimer Adler, and John Dewey. But it was thoughtful of the chairman to sidetrack all that. If I were asked to break a lance tonight in defense of our great tradition I do not think I could display the singleness of aim I once possessed. When I was younger and had my wits about me it was clear that all the ills of American education could be summed up neatly under three points. It had lost its substance three generations ago when our earliest Ph.D.'s brought back from Europe the naturalism they had learned at the feet of Comte and Paulsen and started the drive to remove supernaturalism from American life. It had lost its form two generations ago when Charles Eliot shattered the classical tradition by means of electivism. It had lost its direction more recently through dissemination of a philosophy, manufactured in New York but distributed nationally, which was in substance a blend of pragmatism, socialism and exaggerated experimentalism. In the confusion of old age, however, I have lost the power of neat division and pat answers. I am still a Chicago Montague and would relish the thrill of running a rapier through the gizzard of a Capulet, but the problem now seems too complicated for such an easy solution. Even if our first Ph.D. had not lost God somewhere in Berlin or Paris or even if Dr. Eliot had been able to loosen the grip of classicism on Harvard without knocking American education flat, or even if the Four Horsemen of the Apocalypse could have revitalized teaching without putting the child at the teacher's desk, our problems would not be solved. We should still be facing staggering difficulties.

In fact, these have been such dark and bitter years since 1939 that we should probably apologize to another kind of audience for dwelling on school problems at such a time as this. In the midst of so much disaster, so much destruction of wealth, beauty, life, health, purity, justice and charity, what happens to education may seem to some like a minor tragedy until they realize its bearing on all the rest; until they realize that a great part of the surrounding gloom is due to the absence of intellectual as well as spiritual light. You remember the famous speech made by Viviani in the Chambre des Deputés forty-six years ago when he felt that he had annihilated the Church in France. "This day," he cried, "we have put the lights out of Heaven and they will not be rekindled in our time." It has been left to our day to see the lights of secular learning going out all over the world. On the mainland of Asia the darkness is impenetrable but the twilight in Europe is even more alarming. Europe, after all, has been for two thousand years the source of Western culture—Judean and Greek culture baptized in Eternal Rome—and the universities have been for centuries the storehouses of Europe's thinking. Russia and Germany were casualties before the war, Italy to a less degree. In all of them the discovery and transmission of truth had been distorted to further political ends. In Western Europe where the universities are struggling to rebuild, the planners are plagued not so much by poverty as by the dread of invasion and war. But even if their fears are groundless, even if the United Nations begins to click and Russia reforms and no further troubles develop, how many generations will it take to restore what Europe used to regard as ordinary? Conservationists are worried in this country because four inches of topsoil which were thousands of years accumulating have been washed away since the Revolutionary War. The culture of Europe has lost more than four inches of topsoil, and when will that be replaced?

For ourselves, some extremists in the traditional camp might say that education in the United States was another casualty before the war, but that would be demonstrably misleading. With all our faults we have done some pretty wonderful things in American schools and, although it is a rather terrifying thought, we are at this moment of crisis the hope of the world. Our own needs are many. The economic problem looks large for the private and for some of the tax-supported schools as well. Those of us who worry about deficits of a few thousand may smile when we read that the President of Yale is alarmed because gifts have fallen to $10 million a year. But with inflation and government control on the horizon, why shouldn't he be alarmed? Other needs are even deeper than financial security. We need further clarification of our own thinking and more light on the ultimate aim of education. We need the moral support of a public that will have some insight into our problems and much higher ideals than are revealed by contemporary surveys. But the necessary condition of any real and lasting progress is peace.

The paths to peace are as many and as varied as the paths to war and planning for peace has been a favorite indoor sport for fifty years. Everyone has a pet plan of his own. Unfortunately, however, too many people are thinking only of negative peace. We cannot be content with an armistice, and treaties mean less every day. The peace we must have is a positive thing like health. Health is not just an absence of germs. It is a state which follows order in the functioning of all our members. So Saint Augustine defined peace as "the tranquillity of order." Mortimer Adler in his book, *How to Think about War and Peace,* advanced the thesis that since peace was produced by governments, we could expect universal peace only when we have universal government and that would be in about five hundred years. Where he got the five hundred I do not know, nor do I accept his thesis. Governments make treaties, but the sources of true peace are deeper than government. International peace or the tranquillity that follows international order presupposes national peace, and national order presupposes the order of its component parts, industrial order and domestic order, while they in turn presuppose the order of the individual. We are all familiar with what is meant by "the warfare in our members" and we know there is only one unfailing source of individual order and peace: conformity to the Will of God. To have domestic and industrial order it is not expected that every individual will be at peace, but merely the average man. And so for the national order the average home must be a home of peace, the broken home must be the exception. Obviously if the next generation is to learn this approach to peace we have to do our part in the necessary moral training of the students. The church and the home cannot abdicate and put the whole responsibility on us, but they should be able to count on our cooperation. Nor should they expect us to have a "strong moral commitment" only in Doctor Kilpatrick's sense, which is limited "to the common good and democracy." If we are to work for real peace that starts with personal peace we shall need a strong moral commitment to the praise, reverence and service of God. The Protestant Teachers Association of New York had a communion breakfast last Sunday and Doctor Stokes of Saint Bartholomew's told thirteen hundred schoolteachers that in guiding our youth, the teacher must be as truly a servant of God as a priest or a minister.

For those in private schools such guidance is a matter of judgment and tact. For those in tax-supported schools the difficulties are obvious. We all know the limitations imposed by tradition and still more by a United States Supreme Court that has lost its moorings. But within these narrow limits much can still be done. A teacher's whole manner of life shines through a hundred little crannies of his mind, and no matter what he refrains from saying, his students know in a week that he believes in God and that his ideals are influenced by his belief.

There are then many paths to peace, and some of them call for the cooperation of the teacher. He can, for example, encourage in some the study of history and government. He can develop in others a taste for the literature and philosophy which always tend to dissipate group hates and increase our respect for man as such, no matter what his color, race or creed. He can make sure that his class appreciates at least Doctor Kilpatrick's "strong moral commitment to the common good and democracy." But if he is to attack the question of peace at its root he must realize that peace, the tranquillity of order, begins in his own heart and the hearts of his students and that of all the paths to universal and lasting peace, the surest, if not the shortest, is the conformity of their wills to the Will of God.

An American who was cycling once in southern Ireland lost his way and asked an ancient farmer, "Is this the right road to Cork?" "Faith, it is," said the old man, "and the further you go the righter it gets." That could be said of only one path to peace.

Hate and the Magic of Communication

Catholic Apostolate of Radio, Television and Advertising,
New York, 1958

ORDINARY competition is fair enough, but nothing in my background has prepared me to hold even a captive audience that is looking forward to such excitement. Will you please see to it that they carve on my tombstone the fact that at the age of 102 I finally made the grade and appeared on a program with Hildegarde?

The whole occasion has me breathless. Look at the title of my rambling remarks. It brings back a press conference I once lived through in Japan. My companion at the time was a professor from the University of Salamanca, and for some reason the reporters from several great national newspapers insisted upon a press conference at the hotel in Unzen National Park. The representative of Mainichi in striped pants and morning coat bowed stiffly and said, "Will you two please talk in an intelligent manner for one hour and we shall take notes." I assured him that the professor was the only one present who could talk intelligently on any given subject for ten minutes, and suggested that a few questions might help. The first one was aimed at me. "Discuss please the influence of Buddhism on Japanese character from an American point of view." Fortunately, the professor took over.

This morning, the prospect is a little brighter. I know something about hate and you know all about communication. All we have to do is put our heads together. Evidently the hate we are discussing is not a private violation of charity, but an aberration known as group hate. To hate an individual is bad enough, but to hate a whole group of people is irrational. Old Father Devas, one of the lights of the Farm Street Church in London, used to say, "The only Americans I could ever abide were the ones I had met." And how many of us could say the same thing of other national, racial and religious groups? The ones we happen to know are always "exceptions." This business of group hate is close to our hearts because in the past Catholics have been so hated as a group. You and I may have been lucky enough to have been "exceptions," but now through the magic of communication, the exception is becoming the rule. Group hate is on the way out, at least in America and at least as far as the Catholic Church is concerned.

The Church is projecting its image in America more successfully than America is projecting its image in the world at large. In Europe, America is the land of luxury-loving and unprincipled slobs. In most of the world we are meddling imperialists; in the Moslem world, pure kosher. In return for billions spent in welfare we receive nothing but criticism. Why? Bad communications. Look at some of our unofficial ambassadors. First, our occupation forces. I saw them in Japan in '49 pushing people off the streets. I saw them in Rome in '46 chasing decent women and liberating wrist watches. Then our big businessmen, so expert in stepping on local corns, making no effort to understand the culture of the people they are trying to exploit. Then our missionaries, especially in Latin America, where they spend more time running down the native clergy than they do in building up Christ. Then our entertainers, this disreputable fringe of the motion picture industry which specializes in exporting films that are banned in the United States, and to be banned over here in these sexy times a picture really has to be something. Finally, there is our feature-thirsty press, circulating the wrong magazines throughout the world. Too many of them make a policy of ignoring all the fine men and women we have in public life, in the show business and in sports, to keep the spotlight on a lot of alley cats who are regarded as "typical Americans."

This makes it all the more remarkable that such good communication has been operating in the Church's favor. What more, for example, could the world press, the pictures and TV have done for us at the death of Pius XII and the Coronation of John XXIII? Our younger generation took it all for granted as they do so many other things, but in the lifetime of some people who are still around, a Roman mob attacked the funeral procession of Pius IX with the idea of throwing the Pope's body in the Tiber. Then, when the Cardinals met to elect his successor, the liberals wanted the government to take over the conclave and occupy the Vatican. Fortunately, they were distracted from their purpose by the Turkish War and the death of Victor Emmanuel II. When Leo XIII was crowned, however, there was no representative from the United States of America and the Papal Guard had to protect him from public indignities.

Last month our press, our television and radio brought us every detail of the obsequies which were held for Pius XII and the coronation of Good Pope John. With the burning flax and the wine and vestments, especially the triregnum, it was so medieval that Boniface VIII would have felt right at home, and yet there were 650 sympathetic newspaper correspondents and an army of photographers to pass on a fascinating record to the world. Fifty governments were represented, the U.S.A. by its Secretary of State and its Ambassador to Italy.

What accounts for this tremendous change? More than anything else the march of events, but the magic of communications helped to shape the events. Take three of the principal forces that made things miserable for the Vatican up to a few years ago

—nationalism, French liberalism and religious bitterness. What has happened to them lately? They are still with us, of course. They always will be. But now they are so modified that Good Pope John does not have to give them more than a passing thought.

Nationalism was as potent at the turn of the century as it had been in the Renaissance. People still hated the Pope because he represented an international ideal. Then The Hague Conferences, the ill-fated League of Nations and finally our own controversial United Nations worked a change on public opinion. People began to realize again what they had known so well in the Middle Ages, that they were not only Englishmen, let us say, but members of the human race. This reappraisal of internationalism was sharpened by the lessons of Nazism and Fascism and later still by the madness that began to rise in Africa and various parts of Asia. Because all this had been highlighted by the press and brought by the radio and TV to millions who never read for themselves, the internationalism of the Catholic Church is once more a source of admiration.

So with the second force, French liberalism. We call it that because liberalism can mean so many things—some of them wise and some of them foolish. We limit it here to the irreligious type that was spread by the French Revolution and became so strong especially in the Latin countries. Here in the United States, it came to power largely through the influence of Latin Masonry and its offshoot, the Scottish Rite. When the Church fought back for its life, it was condemned—and not only by the liberals—as antidemocratic.

The reading public feels differently about it now, largely through the magic of communications. It realizes that American and British democracy, unlike that of the French Revolution, is Christian in its origins and perfectly at home in Catholic circles. Cardinal Gibbons, Cardinal Mercier, Cardinal Manning, and above all, Leo XIII, were speaking through the press a language that all free men could understand and the effect of their Christian liberalism is seen in the prestige of their successors.

What shall we say of the third force—religious bitterness? People think of it now as a family skeleton in the closet, dead and best forgotten. They forget how recent was its demise. Not long ago I attended a faculty forum in the University of West Virginia and joked a little about Maria Monk and the Know-Nothings of yesterday. Afterwards, a professor of chemistry, perhaps fifty years of age, came over and said: "Well, sir, we could laugh at those things today, but my father taught me—and I believed him till I was eighteen—that Catholics were dangerous only when they started to be friendly, because every Catholic was pledged to make friends with one Protestant and kill him." His father must have told him that sometime since the turn of the century. It must have been the time of the Lay Laws that banished all religions from France and closed all religious schools.

Now Europe is used to Schumann, De Gaulle, de Gasperi and Adenauer, and over here, I am told, one of our Catholic statesmen thinks he can succeed President Eisenhower. What has happened? It is largely the magic of communications, though a tremendous factor in tempering religious bitterness is to be found in the rise of a militant antichurch movement. Catholics, Protestants and Jews have begun to realize where their real enemy is lurking, and how dangerous it is to weaken any fellow American who is serving God according to his lights.

Above and beyond all this, we are conscious of a special gift from heaven in the character of our modern Popes. They have been without exception moral leaders who needed no defense. They have made it so easy for us to be loyal to them. We never knew the struggle that good Catholics of the past had to face in standing up for some of the notorious Popes of the Renaissance. That does not mean that all in recent years were equally successful in taking advantage of this magic of communications we are talking about. Pius IX, Pius X, and Benedict XV did not project an image calculated to win a critical world. Leo XIII, Pius XI, and Pius XII were eminently popular. The late Pope, as Cardinal Pacelli, toured America and won everybody he met from the President down. As the sovereign Pontiff he received 10,000,000 in audience: 1,200,000 service men and women of a dozen nationalities. Every non-Catholic who met him admired him and transferred part of the admiration to the church he represented.

He was thought to be irreplaceable, but gave us an example to prove that when the Holy Ghost puts His mind to it, there is no such thing as an irreplaceable Pope. In the present Holy Father, we see how widely different men can be equally successful in representing Christ to his Church. John XXIII, Good Pope John, won over the press of the world in forty-eight hours and continued to project the image we have always needed. They loved him in the Balkans and Istanbul. They loved him in Paris. They loved him in Venice. And now with wider horizons he looks bigger than ever but just as amiable. Because of newspapers, magazines, books, radio and television, he will continue to draw souls to Christ in university lecture rooms and lunch wagons, and always with equal ease.

Just think of it! You are his partners. Do you realize how blessed you are in belonging to such an apostolic profession?

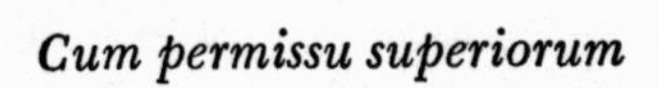

Cum permissu superiorum